Hot Springs and Moonshine Liquor

A History of Illegal Whiskey
in the Shenandoah Valley

Louella Bryant

Black Rose Writing | Texas

©2020 by Louella Bryant
All rights reserved. No part of this book may be reproduced, stored in a retrieval system or transmitted in any form or by any means without the prior written permission of the publishers, except by a reviewer who may quote brief passages in a review to be printed in a newspaper, magazine or journal.

The author grants the final approval for this literary material.

First printing

Some names and identifying details have been changed to protect the privacy of individuals.

ISBN: 978-1-68433-598-5
PUBLISHED BY BLACK ROSE WRITING
www.blackrosewriting.com

Printed in the United States of America
Suggested Retail Price (SRP) $15.95

Hot Springs and Moonshine Liquor is printed in Baskerville

*As a planet-friendly publisher, Black Rose Writing does its best to eliminate unnecessary waste to reduce paper usage and energy costs, while never compromising the reading experience. As a result, the final word count vs. page count may not meet common expectations.

Cover photo: 1930 arrest photo of Virginia bootlegger Willie Carter Sharpe.

For my Nida ancestors

Other books by Louella Bryant

The Black Bonnet

Father By Blood

While In Darkness There Is Light

Two Tracks in the Snow

Full Bloom Stories

Cowboy Code

Hot Springs and Moonshine Liquor

Prologue

My Aunt Hilda hands me a photo of three men sitting on a contraption as big as a caboose. Two large drums connect by a series of pipes. One drum is a type of boiler with a circular door on heavy hinges and an eight-foot-tall stovepipe as round as a man's chest rising from it. Valves and gauges and intricate-looking gadgets top the second drum. Large wagon-type wheels flank the apparatus, and the front is propped with rocks.

"What is it?" I ask Aunt Hilda. She is a devout Christian, a pray-before-meals southern Baptist. And she's a teetotaler.

"It's a still," she says matter-of-factly and points to the man at the front. "And that's your great-great-uncle Bures Paxton."

The two behind Uncle Bures look like teenagers. The one perched by the chimney wears overalls and a shirt rolled to the elbows. He has on a bowler hat with a curved brim. His arms are crossed and there's a slight grin on his face—or maybe it's a smirk. The fellow to his right has on the same outfit, a sort of uniform of the working man. Business casual we might call it today. He's smoking a corncob pipe and wears a homburg, the hat made popular by King Edward VII. The hat sits back on his head, exposing a wide, intelligent forehead. Uncle Bures clasps a curved pipe between his lips and sports a fedora, the fashion for middle-class men in 1920, casual for daytime and stylish for evening. The brim tilts saucily over one eye. Think Humphrey Bogart, gangsters, speakeasies. Bures is thirtyish, the ringleader. Work gloves keep his hands from getting soiled on the machinery. The three men are clean-shaven and stare brazenly at the camera.

"My ancestors made moonshine whiskey?" I ask Hilda.

"Everybody did in those days," she says.

Southwest Virginia where my family lived is the perfect place to set up a business that requires the veil of nature. The George Washington and Jefferson National Forests cloak the counties where my foremothers and forefathers farmed, and the forests sweep over two million acres of Appalachian Mountain land in West Virginia, Virginia, and Kentucky, all the way to the North Carolina border.

Up the road from Buchanan, Virginia, is a rustic cabin my parents bought in the 1960s. To get there, we drove into the Shenandoah Valley, fording a few streams where bridges had not yet been built. Double concrete tire paths just under the water's surface must have been set when the riverbed was dry, and crossings could be done only in summer when the water was not up over the car wheels. My father gunned the Chevy as we entered the river, and watery wings flew from the wheel wells. Those fordings when water sprayed up around the car windows were my favorite part of the trip. We wended our way along Jennings Creek, a tributary of the James River, and crossed railroad tracks, the aroma of metal and moist earth rising up to us. Once we opened up the cabin and settled in for the night, a train's whistle and its baritone clatter on the rails along with the whoosh of the water over the creek's falls lulled me to sleep.

When we first bought the cabin, we had to fight our way through cobwebs dangling from the ceiling beams. Mice scurried through the kitchen. Antiques and dust-covered junk were piled everywhere. The stone fireplace was unusable because squirrel nests clogged the chimney. Moths had eaten holes in the carpet, under which the linoleum peeled and cracked. We swept spiders from casings to pry open windows and let in mountain breezes that chased away the must and mildew. Honeysuckle, pawpaw, fermentation and loam scented the air wafting from the surrounding Blue Ridge Mountains.

Built in 1925 at the height of Prohibition, the cabin showed evidence of lively parties—pictures of movie stars thumbtacked to the walls, a stack of 78 rpm records next to a windup Victrola, and dozens of empty whiskey bottles on the kitchen shelves. They named the place Pine Cliff because of the surrounding conifers and the cliff it perches on. Below the cliff, Jennings Creek cascades over a drop-off into a deep swimming hole.

Once we had the place spruced up, my family enjoyed some good times there, swimming in the stream, hiking along the Appalachian Trail that meanders just yards above the cabin, and playing cards by lanternlight while we listened to the scratchy records. After my parents passed on, my brother Don took over Pine Cliff and now uses it for hosting his buddies on weekends, hunting and trout fishing. Don doesn't drink, but he supports the local economy. Once when I visited him, he opened the door of an old oak icebox, one he took from the Pine Cliff porch and restored. From the lower compartment, he pulled out four gallon-size mason jars filled with suspicious looking fluid. Preserved peach halves nestled on the bottom of the pinkish jar. The other jars held liquid colored with damson plums, blueberries and strawberries.

"What is this stuff?" I asked.

He grinned. "It's moonshine whiskey."

"Where'd you get it?"

He didn't want to reveal his source, but I waggled it out of him. His daughter had been a student at Ferrum College in Franklin County, which author Matt Bondurant calls "the wettest county in the country" in his book titled *The Wettest County in the World*. With relatives in Franklin County, Mr. Bondurant should know. A friend of my niece was paying his tuition by selling jugs of moonshine. Don donated eighty dollars to the boy's scholarship in exchange for the white lightning, twenty dollars for each gallon jar.

He unscrewed the lid of the blueberry jar, its contents half gone. Blueberry appeared to be a favorite. Carefully, he poured a dram of the liquor into a little cordial glass.

"Have a taste," he said.

I'd heard that moonshine can be contaminated with toxins, but I trusted my brother not to poison me. The first swallow was like liquid fire. My throat blazed. My eyes watered. I coughed. I've heard that a single shot of moonshine is like drinking six beers, and I felt the alcohol shooting through my veins. After a few more sips of the firewater, I excused myself and went to bed. The taste of moonshine must learn to be tolerated, but I don't think I'll ever get used to its effect.

The main ingredients of whiskey are corn and barley. For centuries farmers in Europe and the States told stories of John Barleycorn. When the crops were cut down for harvest, John Barleycorn was "killed," so they said, and each planting season he was resurrected. The poet Robert Burns wrote a ballad of Barleycorn: "They took a plough and plough'd him down,/ Put clods upon his head,/ And they hae sworn a solemn oath/ John Barleycorn was dead." John Barleycorn was the demon ministers preached against in their temperance sermons and against which wives of drunkards staged protests. In January 1920, when the Eighteenth Amendment brought on the Prohibition era, John Barleycorn was declared dead for good, and funerals were held across the country for the mythical figure.

My mother's Uncle Shorty saw John Barleycorn's demise as economic opportunity. He fired up his still outside Lexington, Virginia, and smuggled his moonshine to speakeasies in Washington, Philadelphia, and New York, where partiers drank martinis made with his illicit booze. In lower-class neighborhoods where a speakeasy was known as a "blind pig," a proprietor charged admission to see an odd animal—a fictitious blind pig or a blind tiger—and then offered a complimentary drink. It was legal to give the homebrew away, but you couldn't sell it.

As the name moonshine suggests, deliveries were made by the light of the moon. Shorty always had an ear out for federal agents—he called them "revenoors"—who lumbered through the underbrush in search of an illegal still.

Great-uncle Shorty was my grandfather's brother and my mother remembers him bursting into the house one night panting, "Archie, they're after me." Federal agents, he meant. Nandaddy was an honest man who worked as a foreman for the Covington paper mill. Suspecting his younger brother would get into trouble one day, he was ready. The back seat of his Model A Ford lifted up on hinges. Nandaddy emptied out the tire iron and fishing tackle, stuffed Shorty into the compartment—no easy task because Uncle Shorty, who was not an inch above five-five, was as round as he was tall—and settled my mother and her brother on the seat cushion as a decoy. Then he took off, careening around mountain switchbacks through the towns of Healing Springs, Hot Springs and Warm Springs into West Virginia and up through Maryland, not stopping until he arrived in Harrisburg, Pennsylvania, where he pried Shorty out of his cramped compartment, dusted him off, and put him on a train to Kentucky.

When the Twenty-first Amendment was ratified in 1933, ending Prohibition, John Barleycorn rose from the dead. But his revival didn't end the moonshine trade. Too many were making too much money to shut down their stills just because a federal law made whiskey legal. And they weren't inclined to pay a tax on their own merchandise.

The writer Sherwood Anderson lived in southwest Virginia and wrote that it was a gracious country, and it is. If you visit any of my relatives, they'll insist you stay for a meal. And if you're lucky, they'll unearth a mason jar from the root cellar and pour you a shot. Just don't ask where they got the whiskey. Chances are, it came from a still owned by a descendent of one of my uncles. Down that way, they like to keep tradition in the family.

Chapter One ~ Ships at Sea

[A]s an encouragement to them to behave well, and to attend diligently to Their Duty, the Colonel [Washington] promises to give them, so long as they deserve it, four gallons of rum, made into punch, every day.
~ General Orders from George Washington
to Samuel Overton, August 7, 1756

Gadsby's Tavern in Old Town Alexandria, Virginia, takes its patrons back two and a half centuries. Its squeaky wood floor, ceilings framed with crown molding, spindle-back Windsor chairs, and twelve-light windows set deep in brick walls attest to its architectural history. The waitstaff is garbed in billowing sleeved shirts and tight knickers, just as in 1770 when Gadsby's served its first customers.

My husband orders a bottle of the Thomas Jefferson ale, which boasts 8% alcohol. The George Washington ale packs a similar jolt.

"Did the colonials drink beer?" I ask the proprietor.

"Absolutely," he says. He's dressed for our time.

"And where did the beer come from?"

"Washington, Jefferson, Franklin, Hamilton—they all brewed their own."

I told him that I'd heard Washington had a still.

"True," he said. "Our first leaders distilled spirits rather than import it from England. They took their independence seriously."

Apparently they took their booze seriously, too.

In the eighteenth and nineteenth centuries, a tavern was a place where a guest could rent a room for the night—like today's inns. Most every tavern had an "ordinary," a bar where one could get a drink and maybe a bite to eat, and a "necessary" out back, where a fellow went when he needed to relieve himself. Gadsby's calls itself a tavern, although it's more a restaurant. The ordinary is now used for dining tables, and there's no bar to belly up to. The necessaries are upstairs and there are two with modern plumbing.

In Washington's day Gadsby's was a center for political and social life. In the second-floor ballroom, patriots like Washington, Adams, Jefferson and Madison conspired over dinner and ale to free America from England's oppressive rule. There's a southern flavor to Gadsby's menu: Smithfield ham biscuits, crispy fried oysters, and George Washington's favorites—grilled breast of duck with port wine orange glacé and Gentleman's Pye, a red wine stew with lamb and beef. When the waiter asks, I order the salmon. My husband prefers the Meatloaf a la Daube made with beef and veal and comes with a port wine mushroom sauce. It seems the founding fathers liked a bit of alcohol in their food as well as in their tankards.

In its time, Gadsby's was considered the finest public house in America. The food was excellent, and the tavern was a convenient meeting place for Washington and his colleagues. Washington lived eight miles down a road shaded by trees lush with Virginia creeper vines. Every year he celebrated his birthday at Gadsby's and it was at Gadsby's that he took the oath of office as the first president.

My husband and I are here not only to taste the fare but to get a feel for what life was like in the 1700s when my mother's forebears emigrated from Germany. Washington was a teenager when Johann Michael von Nida packed his bags for the journey across the Atlantic. His father was a well-respected baron in Aachen, but Michael, as he was known, had spent his life there and at twenty was ready to break away. Nestled between Dusseldorf and Brussels, Aachen was a vacation spot for both Germans and French-speaking Belgians.

The French called the town Aix-la-Chapelle, or Waters of the Chapel. In ancient times, Romans settled the village so they could bathe in its thermal springs. Charlemagne had a palace built there with adornments of gold and silver, solid brass doors and columns made of Italian marble.

For six hundred years coronations of German emperors were held in the Aachen basilica. Handel and Casanova visited the hot springs. So did prostitutes, who thrived on income from wealthy clientele visiting the baths to soothe their ailments, which included, not surprisingly, an epidemic of syphilis.

From the springs, rolling hills stretch out to distant mountain ranges, and fertile valleys coax wine grapes to juicy fatness. Michael von Nida's father took advantage of the grape bounty by building a stone winery, which operated for 250 years. Why should a family with wealth and prestige leave such a place? Like most of their neighbors, they worshiped in the German Reformed Church, a conservative Calvinist denomination with belief in scripture, grace, and the divinity of Christ. As noblemen, they enjoyed creature comforts and had no need to seek a fortune in the American wilderness. But there was more than wealth on the line.

The War of Austrian Succession had been going on for eight long years. Austria was fighting Prussia over the tiny country of Silesia, located in what is now southern Poland, an area rich in minerals and natural resources. Armies of King Frederick the Great invaded Silesia twice in the 1740s. Michael had too much at stake to go soldiering, and his new wife was due to deliver their first child any week. He wanted his baby raised out of harm's way, so he paid a hundred florins (about $2.50) for two tickets' passage on the good ship *Hampshire* bound for America.

In August 1748 when Michael and his expectant bride Maria arrived at Rotterdam to board the ship, the *Hampshire's* Captain Thomas Cheesman greeted them. When he looked at Maria's swollen belly, he raised an eyebrow. He was a dapper man with a high collar and a frill of lace at the neck. The double-breasted buttons on his captain's coat were made of solid brass. As a ship's commander, he had performed marriages but delivering a child was not his cup of mead. The voyage would take just a month if all went well, but Dame von Nida looked ready to birth her baby at any moment. Most of the seventy-five men aboard were young and unmarried, but a dozen had wives. Surely two or three of the *Frauen* could help with a birth, if it should come to that. First, there was a river to navigate, then the English Channel and the Celtic Sea to cross. Beyond lay the vast Atlantic where they would sail against the wind, tacking and bobbing over ocean billows. Captain Cheesman had his hands full.

Aboard a ship at sea, there is a chill even in summer. At night the passengers shivered under woolen blankets. Maria's underskirt was made of wadding quilted between linen and wool and held in place with fancy stitchery. With the thick layer of clothing and the miniature furnace in her belly, she was plenty warm. They had left the servants and attendants behind, and she had stopped bothering to powder her hair. She was too uncomfortable to be concerned with such vanities.

The *Hampshire* avoided storms to the north and sailed under clear skies. As the ship swayed, several of the Germans lost their stomachs and heaved over the gunwales. Waste buckets, too, were dumped overboard and rinsed with salty sea water. They rationed drinking water, but there was plenty of beer to dull the senses and make the long days seem shorter. In spite of rocking decks and an endless ocean, the parties were in good spirits.

They had been under sail three weeks when in late August Maria's labor pains began. Captain Cheesman wished she'd waited. In another week or two they'd be in Philadelphia, and she could have a whole passel of children if she so desired. At least Maria had carried the baby to full term, which meant she was healthy, a miracle considering the challenge of sanitation. When the baby came, a woman with children of her own tied the cord with a lace thread and cleaned the newborn. Maria von Nida was young—in her late teens—and the baby thrived on her breast milk. He was a little fighter. It was as if he knew that future generations of von Nidas depended on his strength to survive, even in the middle of an ocean. I often feel that hidebound determination pumping through my own heart and give silent thanks for the vitality of my precursors.

By the time the *Hampshire* reached Delaware Bay and sailed up the river to Philadelphia, Johann David von Nida slept cozily in his mother's arms.

Immigration officials required new arrivals to sign the Oath of Allegiance to their new country before they were permitted to leave the ship. The clerk wrote the names of passengers the way they sounded to him. It may be that Michael had contracted a cold on the passage or perhaps he was choked with emotion on reaching America. In any event, the clerk wrote his name as Johann Michael Didah, and Michael didn't bother to correct the spelling—he was just glad to get his wife and son off the crowded ship.

The von Nidas and many of their shipmates settled in Cumberland, Maryland, just a few miles from where sixteen-year-old George Washington was working as a surveyor in Frederick County. While Michael built a modest home and started a family, Washington moved into his half-brother Lawrence's fabulous Mount Vernon estate a hundred fifty miles east of Cumberland.

When Johann David von Nida was just a toddler, sixty-three distilleries had been established in Massachusetts, many of them operated by Puritans. The rum they produced was made with molasses sold to them by slave traders. The traders used the money to buy African natives that they then sold to West Indian sugar planters. Within the first century of its existence, America had already established both slavery and liquor as big business, according to the American Whiskey Trail.

David von Nida was still in his teens when he became a surveyor's assistant. His job was handling the measuring chain, a position held to high standards of honesty and precision. Neither David von Nida nor George Washington could tell a lie, it seems. As "hinder chainman," David, positioned at the starting stake, held the end of a roll of chain and directed a second man to unroll the spool while backing toward the next surveyor's mark. David had to be sure the front man kept the chain in line with the mark, a task that took accuracy and skill. Mistakes meant getting fired, but he was good at his work.

When he wasn't surveying, David helped his father with the farm work. German neighbors lent each other a hand with chores from house and barn raisings to corn shucking, just a few of the opportunities for socializing. A neighbor had a daughter named Mary, a pretty Fraulein who caught David's eye. They sparked, but David wanted to see where America was headed before he took on a wife and family. The previous year, in December 1773, a group of men had disguised themselves as Mohawk Indians and boarded an English ship at Griffin's Wharf in Boston. In protest of Britain's tea tax, they threw 342 chests of London's tea into Boston Harbor. The tea had been valued at ten thousand pounds, the equivalent of two million dollars in today's currency. David worried that the English would retaliate, but he was twenty-six and time was wasting. He turned to Mary and offered her his hand in marriage.

Mary's parents gave David their second-best cow, as was the custom at German weddings. Mary carried salt and bread down the aisle, a tradition believed to bring a bountiful harvest to their marriage. It was also the appropriate time for her mother to pass on the Nürnberg bridal cup to her daughter. The pewter cup comes from a fable centuries old that involves the daughter of a nobleman who fell in love with a young goldsmith. The nobleman refused to give his consent for his daughter to marry a craftsman. When the daughter turned up her nose at the rich suitors and pledged her undying love to the goldsmith, the nobleman had the goldsmith thrown into a dark dungeon. The broken-hearted daughter grew so pale and weak that the nobleman came up with a challenge. If the goldsmith could fashion a goblet from which two people could sip at the same time without spilling a drop of wine, he would give his blessing for the craftsman to marry his daughter. Inspired by love, the goldsmith fashioned an ingenious chalice of a woman, her long hollow skirt to be used as the first cup. Her golden arms were held above her head, and between her hands was a smaller cup set on pins so that it swiveled toward a second drinker when tipped. The goldsmith had met the challenge and claimed his reward—the woman he loved. Today in Germany a version of the wedding cup is used in ceremonies to symbolize love, faithfulness, and luck.

In the absence of wine, the chalice likely contained either rum from Massachusetts or a liquor from Michael von Nida's own homemade creation. The party that followed the wedding ceremony was no doubt joyous and festive.

David settled his wife on his father's farm, and in his spare time he practiced with his firelock until he was a crack shot. If he bagged a rabbit, Mary could skin it in the morning, chop it up, and have a delectable stew on the table by suppertime.

George Washington had also waited to marry. He was twenty-seven when he wed Martha, a widow with four youngsters. When my husband and I visited Mount Vernon and stood in front of the life-sized statues of George and Martha in the lobby of the visitors' center, I was eye-to-eye with Martha and George was exactly my husband's size, six feet two inches. I'd always thought of historical people in two dimensions—just names and images on paper. But here were a famous couple in American history, albeit in bronze, and they looked (except for Martha's tiny tightly laced waist and George's prominent nose) just like us.

In the Mt. Vernon dining room, a tub sat at one end of the table with bottles of what looked to be wine and spirits cooling in fake ice. It appeared that the nation's first president and his wife entertained well. Washington had inherited the eight-thousand-acre estate at Mount Vernon with over a hundred slaves, many of which came with Martha's dower. Female slaves sewed, cooked, and served as well as cleaning stables, clearing stumps from fields, and building fences. The hardest labor was assigned to male slaves, who tended the tobacco and crop fields.

A year after David and Mary pledged their troth, Washington turned his attention to England's assaults on American shores. Ethan Allen and Benedict Arnold had captured Fort Ticonderoga, and King George was ready to teach the rebels a lesson. In defense of the colonies, the Continental Congress formed the Continental Army, a brigade of sixteen thousand motley colonials—farmers, blacksmiths, preachers, and my ancestor David von Nida, who joined the rifle unit. Washington was named general and commander-in-chief, and since none of the men knew anything about soldiering, the general cracked the whip. "Discipline is the soul of an army," he wrote. "It makes small numbers formidable," says the U.S. Army Center of Military History.

Washington applied the lash to the backs of the lazy, the pillory for disobedience, and, for most any offense, the wooden horse—a log affixed horizontally between two posts. The offender had to sit astraddle the log for long, painful hours with weights tied to his ankles. For major infractions, a soldier's head was shaved and his uniform stripped from him, and he was drummed out of camp with insults and dishonor—in his long johns.

As strict as he was with his men, Washington knew that he needed to keep morale high. As the battles intensified, he buoyed morale by providing them with whiskey. While camped in Pennsylvania in 1777, he wrote to a distiller, "[I]t is necessary, there should always be a Sufficient Quantity of Spirits . . . . In many Instances, such as when they are marching in Hot or Cold weather—in Camp in Wet—on fatigue or in working parties, it is so essential, that it is not to be dispensed with," the American Whiskey Trail says. Eventually, the general had his troops set up their own stills along the York County trail in order to be sure his soldiers were fortified with liquid courage.

David von Nida had given his word to be honorable, and he fought staunchly alongside his comrades. He was strong and able and survived not only fierce battles against the British but also the smallpox disease that took half the Continental Army in the north. When the war ended, he went back to Mary in Cumberland. Nearly thirty, he was ready to settle on his own land, and he'd heard that farther south in the Shenandoah Valley there was cheap acreage. Virginia claimed the terrain south of the Ohio River, and its legislators intended to develop it before the French declared it for themselves. David learned that land grants allowed a person to put up a bit of money and plant the fields, and in two years the deed would be handed over to him. Within a year he loaded Mary and their tools and home goods into a Conestoga wagon, its hull like a big ship, its burlap canopy rigged like a white sail. The Mennonite Germans had devised the Conestoga in Pennsylvania fifty years earlier. In wet weather David and Mary and their children could sleep under it to keep dry, and the canopy protected their belongings from the elements. Their hearts were filled with youthful hope as David hitched two of his horses to the wagon and fell in line with his German neighbors, their compass set south along the trail west of the Appalachian Mountains and down the 435-mile Great Wagon Road.

Before the supercontinent Pangaea broke apart and the individual continents drifted away 460 million years ago, the Appalachians were the highest mountains on earth—even higher than the Himalayas today. Over thousands of years the Appalachians have been worn down by the grinding of glaciers, but even today roads in the Shenandoah Valley run north-south rather than east-west over steep ridges. The valley, called "The Great Valley" by white settlers, became the principal migration route from New York to the Carolinas and into eastern Tennessee and Kentucky. Daniel Boone traveled the trail with his family when he was fifteen, coming from his birthplace in Pennsylvania, down through Virginia, and into the back country of North Carolina. Already at that young age Boone was a keen marksman and during their journey kept his parents and siblings well fed with the valley's wild game.

Native people had inhabited Virginia for eighteen thousand years before the first European settlers arrived. Twenty years before David and Mary moved their family into the Shenandoah Valley, the Cherokee had been forced out of southwest Virginia, although the Iroquois were permitted to travel the Blue Ridge to trade farther south. The Paris Treaty that ended the French and Indian War granted lands west of the Allegheny Mountains to the Indians. Although they still hunted in the verdant forests of the Shenandoah Valley, for the most part the natives left the settlers alone.

In 1730, Lord Fairfax owned over five million acres of land in Virginia. Within the next fifty years, the acreage was divided into large parcels which had been surveyed, coincidentally, by the young George

Washington. Under a program titled the Virginia Land Office Grants, a citizen could claim a hundred acres of the land for £40. If no one protested the claim, the property would be deeded to the claimant. David was granted 215 acres which became known as the Niday Tract. Immediately he got behind the plow and planted fields of corn and barley. His taxable possessions were listed as "1 white tithable [a paid servant] and 0 slaves, 3 horses and 5 cattle," Jack Nida reports in the Nida family history. David owned not a single slave.

Jamestown, the first permanent settlement in the New World, was colonized in 1607. Twelve years later, the first slave ship arrived from Africa. Although Virginia claimed ten thousand slaves in 1756, there were none in the Shenandoah Valley until 1750, when the guardian of orphan Ann Jane Usher in Highland County purchased "a Negro girl" to attend to her. Miss Usher grew up with the slave girl, who stayed with Usher even after she married. The two grew old together, and in her will Miss Usher decreed that upon her death the African woman should be freed. When Miss Usher died in 1805, her wish was fulfilled and the slave was given a sum of money and her freedom, reports Oren Frederic Morton in his book, *A History of Highland County, Virginia*.

Unlike his slave-owning commander General Washington, David von Nida economized by harvesting the fruits of his own hard labor. Many of the newcomers wanted homes built like fortresses. They had heard the story of John Smith's near fatal encounter with Powhatan and wanted protection from potentially hostile natives and wild animals. Some houses, like the one my great-grandfather later occupied, were constructed of limestone blocks chiseled to the size of baby coffins. They were unburnable and impenetrable. David built his house of logs from the trunks of heavy oaks harvested from his own land. A rectangle of two and a half stories, it had a gabled roof of wood shingles. For heat, a fireplace and stone chimney stood at each end of the house. The walls were made of plaster and the ceilings a mere six feet one inch high, not tall enough to host George Washington standing straight. The von Nidas were compact and sturdy people. They had made a fine life for themselves, and over the years Mary gave David nine healthy children.

Highway 81 stretches through the Shenandoah Valley from Maryland to Tennessee. Between Front Royal and Waynesboro, the freeway parallels the Blue Ridge Parkway that runs along the crest of the mountains through the forests of Shenandoah National Park. The vistas are breathtaking. I recall elementary school field trips to Luray Caverns and feeling the temperature dip to fifty degrees as I descended two hundred feet underground where water dripped from stalactites into subterranean pools. Virginia's hills harbor four thousand caves, one just a few hundred yards from where David von Nida's house stood. On a knoll is an opening the locals call Murder Hole. Gaping a hundred yards long and sixty yards wide, the hole opens to a pit that descends nearly three hundred feet straight down. Imagine falling from the fourteenth story of a building into pitch darkness.

Murder Hole is a favorite of spelunkers. When explorers enter the cavity, they belay past feathery ferns and jack-in-the-pulpits clinging for their lives to the damp limestone walls. Fog hovers between the warm world above and the cold underworld. Once reaching the soft mud floor, one can wind down a path farther into the cave where stalactites hang in petrified sheets of sediment and the floor sinks again into a deep abyss. Drop a stone into the void and seconds pass before a splash of water echoes back.

The *Roanoke Times* reports that in 1958 one man died when his rope snapped as he was lowering himself into the cave's mouth. Others have had to be rescued. The locals are used to sirens and flashing lights of the fire department pulling out another of the cave's victims. But farther back in time, stories—tall tales, really—circulated about the geological marvel. Supposedly a young couple whose families forbade them to marry drove their horse and buggy off the edge into the deep blackness, choosing to die together rather than live apart.

Tales of Murder Hole vary, but the story responsible for the name involves my ancestor David. The yarn goes that in the late eighteenth century a peddler rode up to David's house in a one-horse jersey wagon—a canvas covered vehicle—and asked to be put up for the night. The von Nidas let him in, and the peddler was never seen nor heard from again. It is suspected that the peddler aimed to rob the family, but he met his match with the von Nidas. Having done in the old peddler, David dragged him to the hole in the ground and pushed him over the edge, so locals believe. The tracks of his horse and wagon led to the brink of the cave, causing neighbors to surmise that the von Nidas tossed the whole operation in after the robber. Hence the name Murder Hole.

My brother Don remembers as a young boy our mother taking him to visit the old Nida homestead and walking out to see the fissure in the earth. Roots of ash and walnut trees border the cave and reach like a thick web across the gaping maw. At night, lights have been seen deep in the hole, suspected either to be ghosts or an illusion produced by phosphorous gas. One man claimed to have seen a skull with horns. Our mother held Don's hand and wouldn't let him get close to the rim, but he says he felt a shudder of awe, imagining that the ground under his feet might rend open and swallow him up.

When the von Nidas cleared the land for their fields, they dumped brush and scrap into the pit along with hundreds of wagonloads of rock. Shortly after making their deposit of stones, the water of nearby Leffel Spring ran muddy, the assumption being that the spring flowed through the underground cave. Had Murder Hole been more accessible, it might have been a clever place to hide a still. But even if David had found an easy way to get in and out of the deep cave, the smoke from his boiler fire might have asphyxiated him. It wasn't worth the risk or the bother.

Most German settlers tended family-run farms—between one hundred and five hundred acres each—and operated them efficiently. But David von Nida had more ambition. Within the next few years he bought 345 acres for £700 ($150,000 in today's money) and added more land until his estate was a thousand acres. Most of the acreage was in the Valley of Sinking Creek, now the Jefferson National Forest. The land was fertile with a long growing season and was furred with enough wood to harvest for buildings and for stove fires. He helped settle a town named Boiling Spring for the hot water bubbling out of the ground. The hot spring pools were used as far back as 7000 B.C.E. by prehistoric people. Washington is believed to have visited these very springs in 1755 and again the following year. David had never been to Germany or seen the baths of Aachen, but perhaps by genetic magnetism he was drawn to this place surrounded by mountains, hot springs, and rich natural beauty.

How did a German immigrant who worked as a surveyor's assistant and served as an unpaid infantry soldier get such a large sum of money to buy a thousand acres of land, not to mention feeding and clothing a family of eleven? Certainly there were no ordinaries for him to frequent in this newly settled territory. If he wanted a drink, he'd have to produce the liquor himself and, while he was at it, he might distill a few extra gallons to furnish his neighbors for a slight remuneration. Several museums in the Shenandoah Valley display stills found in the woods around the settlements, and it is within the realm of possibility that one of them had belonged to my ancestor David von Nida.

While the von Nidas eked out a living from the land, Washington was making a hefty profit in the whiskey business, thanks in large part to a Scotsman named James Anderson. The Scotsman managed Salvington plantation, a 1,700-acre estate near Mount Vernon. With the plantation's twenty-five slaves, he set up a distillery on the property. In Scotland, Anderson had farmed and processed grain for large distilleries, and he knew the industry. Salvington's operation measured a thousand square feet and housed three stills that earned an impressive income for the plantation owners.

But Anderson saw better opportunity in Mount Vernon's grain mills grinding corn, rye and barley. Washington's grist mill was the largest producer of flour in the country, and Anderson approached him for the job of managing the Mount Vernon estate. Washington was impressed with the Scotsman's vision and work ethic and hired him.

Martha had brought considerable wealth into the marriage, and Washington himself was clever with money. By today's standards, they were worth over half a billion dollars—Washington certainly didn't need a distillery to earn money. "Distillery is a business I am entirely unacquainted with," he wrote to Anderson in 1797, "but from your knowledge of it and from the confidence you have in the profit to be derived from the establishment, I am disposed to enter upon one." Washington knew a good thing when he saw it.

Anderson thought big. With the help of his son John and six of Washington's three hundred slaves, Anderson built a foundation of large river rocks taken from the Falls of the Potomac. He had sandstone quarried for the walls. The distillery, which was erected next to the granary, was 2,250 square feet in size—the largest in America at the time. Brick furnaces were built, oak barrels crafted, and copper kettles and piping installed. To Washington's way of thinking, in running the distillery he was practicing the most innovative and creative farming practices of the day. After distilling, the mash was fed to the plantation's 150 head of cattle and 30 hogs, which were happy to have the tasty slop. Nothing was wasted.

Most commonly, Washington's whiskey was made from 60% rye, 35% corn, and 5% malted barley, distilled twice. It had a fruity flavor but was not as sweet as Kentucky's bourbon which has always been 51% corn. Washington preferred a dryer taste, and he drank his fair share, much of it refined into a tasty fruit brandy flavored with apple, peach or persimmon.

The average Virginia distillery produced 650 gallons of whiskey per year. Our guide through the Mount Vernon distillery explained that in 1798 Washington's five stills produced 11,000 gallons of whiskey and profited $7,500 annually—recalculated for today, in the neighborhood of $211,000. Barrels manufactured on the property for storing flour were used to hold the liquor until it could be funneled into gallon jugs to deliver to Alexandria merchants, including Gadsby's Tavern. "Two hundred gallons of Whiskey will be ready this day for your call," Washington wrote, "and the sooner it is taken the better, as the demand for this article in these parts is brisk."

At the time, whiskey cost fifty cents per gallon, but a higher-grade liquor, distilled up to four times, sold for a dollar a gallon. Consumers could pay in cash or barter goods. Washington's best customer was his close friend George Gilpin, who owned a store that sold Washington's whiskey, and other Virginia merchants bought large quantities of the Mount Vernon elixir to resell.

After Washington died in 1799 of a throat infection and loss of blood from multiple bleedings that doctors believed would rid him of the virus, Anderson continued to operate the Mount Vernon distillery. When Martha passed away in 1802, the whiskey business was passed to Washington's nephew, Lawrence Lewis. The Andersons left the area, and Lewis leased the operation to a fellow who let it decline. Stones worked loose from the walls and were taken away for other construction projects. In 1814, what was left of the building burned, and Lewis finagled a modest insurance settlement, our guide explained. It wasn't until the late twentieth century that archaeologists uncovered remnants of Washington's distillery, and in 2007 the building was reconstructed of stones resembling those along the Potomac.

Today Washington's rye whiskey is again being produced. In fact, you can visit the distillery and taste a sample, as we did. A guide in colonial attire will even cheer you with an eighteenth century toast: "Here's to the ships at sea and the ladies on the land. May the former be well rigged and the latter be well met."

As for my ancestor David von Nida, although winemaking ran in his family, in the Blue Ridge Mountains grains were easier to grow than grapes—grains that fermented into a mash that could be distilled into a profitable liquor. A German friend told me that in Germany moonshine is known as *Schwarzgebrannter* from the word "schwarz" meaning black, or black burned. More often "schwarz" refers to the black market—in this case illegally distilled and distributed liquor. If moonshine was good enough for the Washingtons, *Schwarzgebrannter* was surely good enough for the von Nidas.

▪   ▪   ▪   ▪   ▪

Grilled meat was a staple in colonial cooking. Whether it was beef, pork or venison, meat roasted over a fire took on a delicious smoky flavor. To enhance the taste even more, the meat was marinated for several hours or overnight in a sugary sauce spiked with a dousing of whiskey. Here is an updated version of that old standby.

Whiskey Marinated Steak

Prep time: 10 minutes (and overnight marinating)
Cook time: 5 minutes
Ingredients:
2/3 cup water
1/2 cup whiskey
1/2 cup pineapple juice
1/2 cup brown sugar
1/2 cup diced onion
1/3 cup teriyaki sauce
1/3 cup soy sauce
1/4 cup liquid smoke
1 teaspoon minced garlic
4 8-ounce rib-eye steaks

Preparation:
In a medium bowl, whisk together the water, whiskey, pineapple juice, brown sugar, diced onion, teriyaki sauce, soy sauce, liquid smoke, and minced garlic.
Set the steaks in the bottom of a baking dish. Pour the marinade over the steaks. Cover and refrigerate overnight.
Preheat an outdoor grill for high heat and lightly oil the grate.
Grill steaks to desired doneness, 3 to 5 minutes per side for medium rare. Allow steaks to rest for 5 to 10 minutes before serving.
Serves 4.

Chapter 2—War of the Daughter of the Stars

> *If this Valley is lost, Virginia is lost.*
> ~ General Thomas "Stonewall" Jackson leading his Confederate troops to victory in the Shenandoah Valley Campaign.

Visiting the Shenandoah Valley is akin to traveling through time. The Blue Ridge Parkway winds through pristine forests, and as a young girl I remember Sunday afternoon rides when we'd hardly pass another car. In the back seat, my stomach rolled from the rises and falls of the pavement and the curves around rock outcroppings. In the afternoon we stopped at an overlook and took in the view of the valley laced with silver streams and guarded by old mountain sentinels. My mother spread lunch on a picnic table—fried chicken, potato salad, cucumber spears, and ripe, juicy watermelon for dessert. My brothers and I spit the seeds into the woods and wondered if they'd take root and grow fruit-laden vines that crept onto the roadway.

In the sixteenth century Sir Walter Raleigh sent explorers from England to see if the east coast was suitable for colonizing. They encountered Indians who were not always friendly. When the Secotan natives saw the English, they declared "Wingandacoa!"—which means "What good clothes you wear!" The word, says a history of the Lost Colony of Roanoke, may have inspired Queen Elizabeth to name the area Virginia, a nod to her status as the Virgin Queen.

Originally Virginia claimed most of the east coast from Cape Fear northwest into inland Canada, including North Carolina and a triangle of South Carolina, Kentucky, West Virginia, parts of Tennessee, Maryland and Pennsylvania. As the states set up their boundaries,

Virginia held onto its coastline, its section of Appalachian Mountains, and the beautiful Shenandoah Valley.

The name Shenandoah has a sketchy etymology, but I fancy the romanticized version, a Native American expression for "beautiful daughter of the stars." On a night walk in the valley, the sky is so deep and dark and studded with a million twinkling lights that one is struck silent. Locals claim to have seen UFOs and believe aliens live in some of the hundreds of caves along the ridge. And why not—surely aliens could see the advantages of setting up camp in so remote and picturesque a landscape.

I can imagine my great-great-grandfather James Nida—the "von" had been dropped in the previous generation to make the name sound more American—sitting on his porch in Boiling Spring after a day of work on the farm. He and his wife Eliza might have been enjoying a glass of an intoxicating liquid, both growing pensive as they gazed at that same sparkling universe. Jim Nida had earned that hour of peace.

In 1856, Jim could see the gathering storm when Preston Brooks, congressman from South Carolina, launched his mean-spirited attack on Charles Sumner, senator from Massachusetts. In his college years, Brooks had been expelled for brandishing a gun at local police officers. He had a taste for liquor, a vain sense of personal honor, and a propensity for bullying anyone who crossed him. It was his third year in congress when Brooks listened to blue-blood Bostonian Sumner rail against slavery, calling it a "harlot" and implying that slave owners raped their female slaves. Brooks was enraged not only with Sumner's metaphors but with his abolitionist message. If slavery were abolished, southern economics would suffer.

After the speech, Brooks limped onto the Senate floor, leaning on his gold-tipped cane. He had been shot in the hip ten years earlier during a duel with a Texas senator over insults they had traded. Fellow South Carolina congressman Laurence Keitt stood guard at the door with a pistol in his pocket as Brooks approached the desk where Sumner was working over a stack of papers. Sumner, a Harvard man, had a thick head of wavy hair and a fierce look in his eyes. Brooks railed against the speech, but Sumner had stated his beliefs and he wasn't going to apologize for offending this boorish southerner. As he started to stand, Brooks swung his cane and struck him over the head. Sumner staggered. Brooks hit him again—and again. Sumner's head was bleeding, the blood trailing down his forehead and blinding him. He collapsed, but Brooks continued the bludgeoning until his cane broke. When other senators tried to help, Keitt pulled out the pistol and shouted, "Let them be!" Finally, Sumner lay crumpled and unconscious, and Brooks turned and coolly hobbled away.

Sumner survived, but it was three years before he was able to return to his Senate duties. Members of Congress began carrying firearms and knives into their chambers to protect themselves. Northerners condemned Brooks as a brutal coward. Southerners cheered him as a hero.

Jim Nida did not own slaves. He and his brothers worked the family farm, alongside their father, tending livestock and coaxing vegetables from the ground. He loved the Shenandoah Valley and the rich acreage that would one day be his, and he was willing to put his life on the line to defend it.

Two hundred miles to the north, the abolitionist John Brown had launched a raid on the federal armory at Harpers Ferry. When the slaves he planned to arm for revolt failed to show up, Brown was taken prisoner, tried and found guilty of murder, inciting a slave insurrection, and treason against the Commonwealth of Virginia. Then he was hanged.

Jim was twenty-one years old in the winter of 1860 when South Carolina, fearful that its slaves would take to heart Brown's attempt against their masters, seceded from the Union. The following April, just after Jim's twenty-second birthday, Virginia followed by passing a secession bill by a vote of 88 to 55. Now he was paying close attention. The Nida home in Boiling Spring was in the heart of the Shenandoah Valley and if war broke out, the valley would be crucial geography for both sides.

In the North, men between eighteen and forty-five were drafted into the Union army. Until they could acquire uniforms, soldiers wore the costumes of their native countries. Scotsmen and Irishmen fought in tartan kilts. The South gathered a crew of motley-attired volunteers—farmers who left their fields, moonshiners, fathers and sons, some of the men barely old enough to shave.

Not all young men were inclined to risk their lives in the Civil War. According to Jack Nida's genealogy report, Jim's nephew Hiram Nida went west with his brother Henderson rather than put on a uniform. They were in their thirties when the two settled in southern Oregon, where they thought they would be left in peace to pan for a few nuggets of gold. As luck had it, they faced another battle—this one not over slavery but over land. The Rogue River Indians were not willing to give up their wilderness to white men who overhunted the wildlife, overfished the rivers, and cut down entire forests of oak trees. The Nida brothers had jumped from the frying pan into the fire. They found no respite out west, and both died mysterious deaths shortly after arriving in Oregon. If they were victims of foul play, no one was willing to speak. Hiram and Henderson might have done better to gamble their fate on the Civil War battlefields.

In Virginia Jim Nida stood his ground. He said goodbye to his family, kissed his girlfriend Eliza Persinger and promised that he'd return with all his parts intact. By then, the Confederate army had gray uniforms, blue for Union soldiers. Jim donned gray. He was strong and healthy. Eleven years earlier, both he and Eliza had survived the cholera epidemic, the disease thought to have been carried on ships from Europe where countries were paralyzed by the sickness. Former President James Polk died of cholera. In fact, between 1832 and 1849, 150,000 Americans succumbed to the disease. Jim and Eliza had also avoided tuberculosis, which was known as the "White Plague" and had recently taken the life of Henry David Thoreau. Jim felt lucky—lucky enough to tempt fate yet again as a Confederate soldier.

He was assigned to General Jubal Early's 60th Virginia Regiment. Early was from Franklin County, Virginia, twenty miles southeast of

Roanoke. Franklin County, even in the nineteenth century, was known for its moonshine stills. A man could earn a lot more money from distilled liquor than he could from tilling the soil, and at one point most of the Franklin County population was involved in producing or distributing illegal liquor. The county men took ruthless measures to defend their enterprises, and they were quick to arm themselves against attacks from the north.

General Early was a taskmaster and not out to win a popularity contest with his men. He was harsh on them, and his expectations were as high for himself as they were for his infantry. When he took a lead ball in the shoulder, he got one of his men to help him mount his horse so he could keep fighting. He believed in the cause of the South and in his autobiography declared, "Reason, common sense, true humanity to the black, as well as the safety of the white race, required that the inferior race should be kept in a state of subordination." Slavery was the condition that God had intended for a "barbaric race," Early stated. Even so, although Early never married, he kept a black woman, Julia McNealey, in a house near his Franklin County home. When he was on leave, Julia served him supper at her house and later joined him in the room he rented at a nearby tavern. Julia was barely sixteen years old when she gave birth to Early's first child—he was thirty-four—and she would have three more of his children before the war ended. Years later, Early withdrew his statement denouncing the African race and issued a public apology.

Jim Nida had as much at stake as his general in defending the Shenandoah Valley. Strategically, the valley was the back door for Confederate raids on Maryland, Washington, and Pennsylvania. The lush land also kept the soldiers supplied with grains, fruits, and vegetables. In his memoirs, Union General Ulysses S. Grant wrote, "The Shenandoah Valley was very important to the Confederates because it was the principal storehouse they now had for feeding their armies about Richmond. It was well known that they would make a desperate struggle to maintain it." The year my great-great-grandfather enlisted, Stonewall Jackson staged a campaign in the Shenandoah Valley, and the following year General Robert E. Lee led his soldiers between mountain ridges up to Gettysburg. In order to win the war, the valley had to be kept open.

By the beginning of the Civil War, battle technology had evolved from the rudimentary weapons of the Revolutionary War. Whereas ninety years earlier muskets were handmade, by 1860 Springfield rifles and Colt revolving rifles were being mass-produced. Breech-loading rifles allowed soldiers to fire lying down instead of standing. Oliver Winchester was producing a new repeating rifle, which meant a man could fire from horseback because he didn't have to reload after every shot. The smoothbore musket used during the Revolution could kill at 70 yards, but the new rifled musket could hit its mark at 300 yards, according to the American Battlefield Trust.

Being hit with a musket ball was serious business. At makeshift hospitals, there was no way to clean instruments, and surgeries were often more deadly than wounds. Many soldiers who survived the battlefield got infections from dirty knives and bandages. If gangrene set in, doctors cut off the malodorous arm or leg rather than let a patient die. But there were worse fates than lead balls. Many who weren't wounded died of disease, starvation or brutality in prisoner of war camps. What they wouldn't have given for an anodyne of liquor.

Battalions were lucky to get a taste of whiskey. When men left their stills to fight, women took over production and delivered jars of their distilled beverage to the encampments. The alcohol was used as antiseptic and anesthetic, for courage, and for escape from the ugliness of war.

The Civil War was long and blood-spattered. When not in combat, men drilled. When drills were finished, they were left to their own devices. The army banned enlisted men from purchasing alcohol, but the threat of punishment was little deterrent. A company in Mississippi injected liquor into watermelon rinds and sneaked the fruit into their tents. When they were camped for a period of days, troops bought jars of moonshine from local distillers when they could, and when they couldn't, they made their own from anything they could find, including turpentine or lamp oil tempered with brown sugar. A Confederate soldier wrote to his family, "If there is any place on God's fair earth where wickedness 'stalketh abroad in daylight' it is in the army." Confederate General Braxton Bragg echoed that concern: "We have lost more valuable lives at the hands of whiskey sellers than by the balls of our enemies."

Liquor brought out the worst in men, but drinking was not restricted to enlisted soldiers. Union General William Sherman, who served under General Ulysses S. Grant, once said, "Grant stood by me when I was crazy, and I stood by him when he was drunk." In 1854, at the end of his first tour of military service, Grant had been assigned to a company in California. Rufus Ingalls, Grant's fellow soldier and friend from West Point days, reported: "Captain Grant, finding himself in dreary surroundings, without his family, and with but little to occupy his attention, fell into dissipated habits, and was found, one day, too much under the influence of liquor to properly perform his duties," according to biographer Hamlin Garland. The bleary-eyed Grant was turned in to the commanding corporal, who ordered him to resign or stand trial. His father wrote letters to newspapers defending his son but in a letter to his father, Grant wrote: "To say that I have not been distressed at these attacks upon me would be false, for I have a father, mother, wife and children who read them and are distressed by them; and I necessarily share with them in it," Garland reports. In a noble gesture, Grant turned in his uniform and returned to civilian life. But when the Civil War broke out, Grant took up the blue uniform of the Union army. By now he was a robust man who kept his hair closely cropped and his beard neatly trimmed. Unfortunately, liquor continued to have a powerful effect on him. It is claimed that he lost the battle of Shiloh because he was sloshed.

Alcohol had become part of everyday American life. The average adult consumed in excess of five gallons of whiskey a year, much of which he made himself. Liquor was preferable to water from streams that ran through farmlands and carried waste from livestock and grain fields—at least consumers knew what was in the distilled liquids.

Alcohol was thought to be nutritious, and a shot or two stimulated digestion and helped wash down food that was poorly cooked, greasy, salty, or rancid. Whiskey was particularly helpful for relaxing the nerves after tilling the fields. And during the Civil War, a strong drink was an elixir following a day of fighting.

In spite of salacious behavior among the troops, women were drawn to the idealistic peril of fighting for a just cause. Author Catherine Clinton writes of groups of women who named themselves "vivandieres" after those who aided soldiers in the French Napoleonic wars. They were wives or girlfriends with fierce loyalty to the men they loved and to the cause of their side. Willing to brave the dangers of the battlefront, the vivandieres followed the troops, cooking for them, nursing their wounds, laundering their uniforms, procuring goods and liquor for them, and often serving as their prostitutes.

Two women in Jim Nida's regiment, cousins Mary and Molly Bell, cut their hair short and signed on as Tom Parker and Bob Morgan. They lowered their voices an octave, put on thick woolen shirts to hide their bosoms, and walked with a practiced swagger. Both women had grown up on farms and could ride and shoot like men. Twenty-four-year-old Molly, historian Rosemarie Skaine writes, was on guard duty one night when Union soldiers launched an attack on Early's camp. She signaled the alarm and managed to kill three Union soldiers with a muzzleloader before the infantry had their pants on. Because of her heroism, Molly was promoted to sergeant. Mary, who was just seventeen, became a corporal. Each was commended for battle skill and dedication, and their fellow soldiers knew them as first-class fighting men—and most likely drinking men as well. Molly and Mary managed to keep their gender a secret for two years of service in General Early's infantry until fellow soldiers discovered their identities. When the duo were arrested in 1864, Molly claimed that she knew of six other women disguised as men in General Early's ranks. Nevertheless, the cousins were sent to prison for "aiding in the demoralization of General Early's veterans."

Soldiers on both sides found notoriety either for heroism or scandal. Author Steve Robinson writes of Devil John Wright who was known for having the blackest heart in Appalachia. He was sixteen when he joined the Confederate army and rode with Quantrill's guerrilla battalion, a mixed bag of Virginia and Kentucky criminals, mountain men, intellectuals, and misfits who terrorized civilians and Yankees alike. When the company faced off against Ohio regular Union troops, Wright was captured. The Yankees gave him a choice—fight for their side or face the gallows. He shrugged off his gray uniform and put on a blue coat. A Confederate ball to the stomach almost killed him, but he recovered and took up his rifle again. In Tennessee the Rebels got him in the right arm and the left hip. The arm healed, but for the rest of his life he walked with a stiff gait.

When Wright was discharged from the Union army, there was a meanness to him. An incorrigible liar and braggart, Wright carried a pistol that he swore was a gift from outlaws Frank and Jesse James. At other times he claimed he'd taken the gun off a dead Yankee soldier along the Mississippi River. No matter where he got it, he'd just as soon use the pistol to plug a man through the heart as argue with him. His moonshine operation was reputed to yield a liquor of excellent quality, and he taught his sons to manage the stills, which brought in a sizeable income. He gambled and drank and reportedly shot twenty-eight men in gunfights. No one challenged him.

Off the battlefield, it was hard to tell law officers from outlaws. A wrong word and one might find oneself in a fist fight or a gun battle. Feuds broke out at the slightest provocation and often ended badly. The most famous feud was between the Hatfields of western Virginia, who fought for the South, and the McCoys of Kentucky, whose sons were Union soldiers. The death toll on both sides tallied a dozen in hostility that went on for thirteen years.

Virginians west of the Allegheny Mountains, including the Hatfields, were at odds with their Shenandoah neighbors. They didn't appreciate the law giving voting rights only to those owning at least twenty-five acres of land. They also balked at western Virginia aligning itself with the north, even though most of the Shenandoah Valley was controlled by Confederate troops. Nerves were raw in the wake of Nat Turner's slave rebellion in Southampton, and in 1863, despite lack of approval by the state legislature, politicians in the northwest section of Virginia formed an alternative government and ratified the statehood of West Virginia. Jim Nida lobbied to keep land in the Shenandoah Valley, including his own town of Boiling Spring, on the Virginia side of the state line. The land had been his dream and he was a Virginian, heart and soul.

But Jim's valley was being threatened. Union troops stormed in to block Confederates from attacking Grant's battalion advancing toward Richmond. Cadets from Virginia Military Institute in Lexington saw an opportunity to put their martial studies into practice. According to the VMI website, a troop of 257 boys, the youngest just fifteen, marched eighty miles north to New Market, where they joined forces with the Confederates. In a drenching rain, the cadets led the charge across a newly plowed wheat field that became known as the "Field of Lost Shoes" because of the mud that came up over their ankles and sucked off their boots. Barefoot, they captured a Union cannon and turned it on the northern regiments, driving them out of the valley.

It was a short-lived victory for these green fighters. Within a month, the north, under the command of Major General David Hunter, sent 18,000 Union troops onto VMI's Lexington campus. The outnumbered Confederates retreated, and VMI cadets fled into the Blue Ridge Mountains. From a mountaintop they watched as Union soldiers set fire to their barracks, two faculty residences, the library, and the science laboratory. Hunter's men took over the state arsenal housed on campus and stole VMI's statue of George Washington, then advanced across the mountains to Lynchburg. There, on June 17, 1864, General Jubal Early's Virginia infantry and my great-great-grandfather awaited them.

Corporal Nida had fought bravely in the Seven Days' Battles in Richmond in which twenty thousand Confederate soldiers were killed, and he had avoided being among the thousand captured at the Battle of Piedmont. He was indeed one fortunate—or very cautious—soldier. And his luck would have to stand one more time at Lynchburg.

Early's company was known as "The Army of the Valley." The tiny force of nine thousand had threatened armies at Baltimore and Washington and had set fire to the town of Chambersburg, Pennsylvania. General Lee had nicknamed Early "Lee's Bad Old Man" because of his short temper and his fierce military tactics. It didn't take long for Hunter to see firsthand how Early had earned the moniker. Scrappy and bellicose, the Confederates surprised Hunter's army with their grit and aggression. Thinking his battalion was outnumbered, Hunter retreated.

At Christmas Jim took leave and went home to Boiling Spring. He spent most of his time with Eliza and promised that if he came back from the war alive, he'd marry her. After heavy courting and a well-earned rest, he returned to Early's company and prepared for the hardest combat of his life at Waynesboro, less than a hundred miles from home. It was also to be Jubal Early's final battle. His men were low on ammunition and food, and so many soldiers had deserted that the company was a shadow of its former force. But those who remained kept their chins up and their rifles oiled and loaded.

March 2, 1865, brought a cold downpour that muddied the roads. General Sheridan had ordered his Union soldiers to destroy crops and decimate fields to keep farmers from planting—fields of corn and barley that not only fed the Shenandoah Valley's citizens but also provided the makings for a tasty mash on its way to liquor. Destroying those fields meant starvation and deprivation for the valley's armies. "If the war is to last another year," Sheridan said, "we want the Shenandoah Valley to remain a barren waste." The Rebels were weak with hunger. Cans of pork and beans had been distributed to Union troops, but Sheridan made sure that no provisions were available to the Confederates and vowed that even crows flying over the valley "will have to carry their provender with them."

During the standoff at Waynesboro, Sheridan's troops sneaked up Early's right flank, scattering his men. The Yankees picked them up one by one and took them captive. Fifteen hundred men were marched three hundred miles to Fort Delaware, a pentagon-shaped fortress on an island in the Delaware Bay where they would be held until the war ended. Using his wits, Corporal Nida had escaped capture.

After Early's defeat, control of the Shenandoah Valley fell into the hands of the Yankees. Six months later, the Rebels were worn out from battle. General Lee met with General Grant in the Virginia village of Appomattox Courthouse, and after two hours of negotiation, Grant accepted Lee's surrender, bringing four years of bloody war to an end.

Corporal Nida received an honorable discharge and, as he had promised, went home unscathed. Eliza was waiting, her belly growing large with Jim's child. On March 30 the two lovers exchanged vows, and six months later, Eliza gave birth to my great-grandfather, John Henry Nida.

When the Civil War ended, over 600,000 people—one out of every fifty Americans—had given up their lives in battle. Jubal Early pronounced, "I cannot live under the same Government with the Yankee." He disguised himself as a farmer and fled to Mexico and then to Canada, the U.S. History site reports. When things cooled down, he returned home to Franklin County and settled into the practice of law.

As for Jim Nida, he focused on repairing the devastation wrought during the war. Homes had been burned and fields ruined. Recovery was slow, but he persevered and got his farm operating again. He and Eliza reared their nine children and taught them how to eke an honest living from the land. Following Thoreau's pronouncement that most men "lead lives of quiet desperation," Jim did not ask for much. If he made a little moonshine—most everyone in Boiling Spring did—it was for sociability rather than greed.

From a distance, my great-great-grandfather watched World War I transpire, but by that time he was an old man and more concerned with the events around his property than across an ocean. When he was eighty, he died with a clear conscience.

The sons and daughters of Corporal James S. Nida laid him in a handmade coffin and put the coffin on the back of a wagon. They drove the horses up the Shenandoah Valley to Covington and buried him in

Lone Star Cemetery. It seemed a fitting place for the man who loved his family and the land that had nurtured him.

■　■　■　■　■

During the Civil War, most soldiers ate hardtack, a biscuit made of flour that looked like a large soda cracker. Factories in the North baked hundreds of these biscuits every day and shipped them out in wooden crates via wagon or rail. More often than not, the biscuits were in route for a month or more and became so hard that the soldiers called them "tooth dullers" or "sheet iron crackers." If they were infested with weevils, they were known as "worm castles" because of the holes the little vermin bored into them. A soldier was allocated six to eight crackers for a three-day ration, and he would crumble them into coffee to soften them or soak the hardtack in water and fry it in bacon grease. "Skillygallee" was a dish of fried salted pork with crumbled hardtack, a palatable meal for a cold, wet warrior returning from a day of battle.

A sympathetic Irish wife took pity on her husband's stomach (and his teeth) and delivered her soldier a loaf of whisky soda bread to remind him of his homeland. Irishmen were the most opinionated and contentious of immigrant groups in the nineteenth century. Although most aligned themselves with northern sentiments, Jefferson Davis paid homage to the many Irishmen who fought in his regiment. The following recipe for whiskey soda bread honors the "fighting Irish" and their long love affair with that distilled beverage.

Whiskey Soda Bread

Prep time: 10 minutes
Cook time: 50 minutes
Ingredients:
1 cup raisins
1/2 cup Irish whiskey
3 cups all-purpose flour
1/2 cup sugar
1 tablespoon baking powder
1 teaspoon salt
1 tablespoon grated orange rind
1/2 teaspoon baking soda
1-1/3 cups buttermilk
1/4 cup butter, melted
Whiskey Butter:
1/2 cup butter, softened
1 tablespoon Irish whiskey

Preparation:
Soak raisins in whiskey overnight.
Preheat oven to 350 degrees.
For a half cup whiskey butter, blend whiskey with softened butter and set aside. For bread, combine flour, sugar, baking powder, salt and orange rind in large bowl, mixing well. Stir in raisins and whiskey. Dissolve baking soda in buttermilk and stir into flour mixture. Add melted butter and mix well. Spoon batter into greased 2-quart casserole dish.
Bake for 50 minutes or until golden brown.
Cut into squares and serve with whiskey butter.
Yield: 8 to 10 servings.

Chapter 3—A Culture of Contrasts

Whiskey isn't the only thing that's been distilled in these hills. The people are a distillation, too ... refined by mountain summers and winters and condensed by hard times.
~ Charles Kuralt

In Covington, Virginia, the Blue Ridge Mountains rise mossy and misty, ground down by time like old teeth. The hills still bear scars where the paper company cut timber, gray smoke spouting from the chimneys of the company's mill as it turned wood into cardboard. The sky layers itself in pink and blue over Oliver Mountain and the sun rests in the notch of Fore and Lick Mountains, shining pewter on the Jackson river.

Two hundred years ago you might have seen a broken plow frame rusting in a meadow of chopped cornstalks, a hen roost of unpainted pine, a crusty pile of horse manure in the road. Laundry would be hanging on a line—sheets straight as walls, a pair of dungarees, men's shirts upside-down, arms dangling beneath them. Clothes were left on the line just long enough to dry, then unpinned and folded before the mill's soot settled on them. On a porch, a spindle-back chair, a broom with bristles worn to a slant. Beside the chair, the ubiquitous jug of moonshine.

Settlers in Appalachia came seeking freedom to bear arms, to reconcile their own disputes, and to generate their hooch without taxation. They were a thirsty lot, and liquor was one of the few comforts in their new homeland. These noble rustics had a hand in designating corn liquor the first truly American whiskey.

After the Revolutionary War, when Treasury Secretary Alexander Hamilton expressed worry that the new nation was far too enamored with what he called "ardent spirits" because of its cheap availability, drinking farmers balked, says Michael Veach in his book *Kentucky Bourbon Whiskey, An American Heritage*. Hamilton reasoned that if he put a tax on liquor, he could curb its use, improve the health and morality of the country's citizens, and at the same time plump up the Treasury coffers. Such a tax, he said, would create an effect "in every respect desirable." But he didn't say desirable to whom.

Hamilton wasn't completely opposed to alcohol, having thrown back a few drinks in his day. For agricultural economics, he considered "cyder" and malt liquors more profitable than distilled liquor. In fact, Hamilton believed malt liquors increased the vitality of the citizens and, according to sources at Gadsby's Tavern, his personal preference was a malt brew over a distilled one.

President Washington agreed to Hamilton's tax, convincing himself that he wasn't taxing the citizens directly. But after a hard day in the fields or the factories, locals had a thirst that could only be quenched with whiskey. Water running out of the mountains was muddy after a rain and had to be filtered for leaves, pollywogs, and other debris. They preferred to drink liquor because they knew the ingredients—they had made it themselves.

A tax was an affront to the lifestyle and well-being of Shenandoah Valley people. When a tax collector came around, whiskey makers tarred and feathered him, set fire to his house, or hanged him from a tree and left the swinging body as a warning. But the tax wasn't any more welcome in other parts of the new republic. In Pittsburgh, violence erupted in the streets, and Washington sent in 13,000 troops, more than had fought in the battles of the Revolution, to control what came to be known as the 1789 Whiskey Rebellion.

Groups protested in Maryland, Virginia, North Carolina, South Carolina, and Georgia. Federal agents didn't even attempt to collect the tax in the territory of Kentucky. Distillers there were armed with muskets and ready to use them against trespassers, even if the agents were on the government's payroll. Several counties in Pennsylvania and one in Virginia flew flags of independence and threatened to secede over the tax. When Washington initiated a draft recruiting soldiers to quell the disturbances, more riots and protests broke out against the conscription. In towns and along roads, whiskey tax rebels planted liberty poles like those raised during the Revolution. It appeared that the young nation was again at war.

The tax held until Jefferson took office. It was believed that whiskey drinkers elected Jefferson on his promise to repeal the liquor tax. He made good on that pledge, declaring the tariff "infernal" and "hostile to the genius of a free people," according to the Bureau of Alcohol, Tobacco, and Firearms.

Nowhere were citizens more relieved to be rid of the tax than in the Shenandoah Valley. In the early twentieth century, when times were hard great-grandfather John Henry Nida looked to his wife's nephew Bures Paxton to help out, and Bures was glad to do it. Powered by a steam tractor, Bures's still supplied homemade whiskey to Boiling Spring and Covington residents, and business was so brisk that he hired a couple of boys to keep the still operating around the clock. Bures may have delivered jars of his homemade elixir to Roanoke, but he dare not venture into nearby Franklin County. The Bondurant family controlled the business there and it was hazardous to infringe on their territory, according to author Matt Bondurant, a descendant of the notorious bootleggers. Hooch-makers did not take kindly to strangers of any sort and were known to have a pistol tucked in a belt and a dagger in a boot. If you weren't a revenuer, a distiller might think you were taking a bit of cash under the table to snitch on a neighbor. Such a betrayal could bring on a confrontation in which someone was almost assured to be hurt, tortured or killed. Besides, so many citizens of Franklin County made whiskey themselves, including politicians, law enforcement officers, and preachers, that Bures Paxton figured he'd be foolish to go where he wasn't welcome.

Bures's steam tractor was mobile, and so was his whiskey operation. If the Feds wanted to arrest him for operating an illegal distillery, they'd have to find the thing first. Revenuers would be looking for a telltale curl of chimney smoke coming from the forest, but Bures burned juniper, gum and walnut because those woods were easy to split and didn't give off much smoke.

Police and moonshiners played elaborate games of cat-and-mouse. Stills were camouflaged with brush or crude fences woven of sticks and leaves. They were set up in abandoned sheds, underground dugout rooms, or unused cemetery plots. According to a gentlemen's code, a revenuer could arrest a bootlegger only if he was caught red-handed making or selling liquor. A Rocky Mount lawyer defended one moonshiner who was caught when agents spied on him with binoculars. The defendant complained, "It ain't fair. They didn't see me with the naked eye," reports Keister Greer in his book, *The Great Moonshine Conspiracy Trial of 1935*.

John Henry Nida had his hands full with his wife Annie Elizabeth and their eight children, among them my grandmother, Lucy Ethel. Ethel, as she was called, was sent to high school in Covington, fifteen miles north along meandering Potts Creek Road. She was kin to most everyone in the village of Boiling Spring, but Covington was a big town and the larger pond had more fish. Among those fish was Archer Bush, a compact and shy young man who flashed his blue eyes at her. He was fair, not like the dark-haired Germans of Boiling Spring. She married him at Bures's house. Bures and his wife Aleah signed the marriage certificate and offered toasts with his best homemade tonic.

Bures was an entrepreneur in many areas, including real estate, and he helped settle the newlyweds into one of his rental houses on Covington's Spruce Street, where Fore Mountain rose from the back yard to its three-thousand-foot-summit. For the little good it did, Archie fenced the yard to keep foxes and panthers from the chickens. Everyone knew the story of the woman riding her horse between the railroad tracks and the forest when a panther with a taste for blood came out of the woods and startled the horse. It reared up and threw off the woman, who hit her head on a jagged rock. The horse galloped away, and the panther turned its attention to the screaming woman. Even now, night visitors to Panther Rock claim they can hear the woman's cries for help and the panther's bone chilling shrieks. When it rains, they say, the rock turns red and an eerie quiet settles over the site.

Covington was named for a hero in the War of 1812, and in the early years the town was a sparsely populated agricultural community with a few businesses that depended on farmers who tilled the soil and raised livestock. Railroad tracks curve around the steep slopes of the mountains, cross the Jackson River, and wind through the middle of town. By the late nineteenth century, industries had established themselves within the town borders. The Covington Iron Furnace produced a daily output of 110 tons of pig iron. There was a tannery, a lumber mill, and a machine factory that made coke extractors used to fire furnaces in steel mills. Two flour mills, two brickyards, and the Alleghany Pin and Bracket Company employed a high percentage of the town's citizens. In 1900 West Virginia Pulp and Paper Company built the paper mill, which brought more jobs to the town, but pollution became an unfortunate byproduct. The runoff from the mill dumped directly into the Jackson River. Boys were urged not to fish in the water, clogged and yellow with mill refuse.

The mill churned out containers for everything from appliances to laundry soap, and people across America poured their morning cereal from boxes made in Virginia's Blue Ridge Mountains. Cardboard and newsprint were spooled onto heavy rolls that forklifts stacked end-to-end in towers.

Accidents were a regular occurrence. In a split second a finger or arm could be sliced off in a cutter. The dangers were prodigious—being crushed by a paper roller, burned by hot slurry, deafened by the racket, or broken by a fall.

In 1940 my mother's first husband, Walter Vanness, wanted to join the army but he had his wife and their two boys to support. The paper mill gave him enough salary to live on, and he set down roots in Covington. As he did every day, he climbed a high ladder to check the seams on a drum, a furnace as tall as a silo that heated wood chips into pulp for papermaking. Before firing up the furnace, the seams had to be tight. The boilers built up volatile gases, and a leak in the solder could be disastrous. Van, as he was called, saw that one seam had a little bubble that needed fixing. The night before, he had been out with his buddies and had drunk his fair share of moonshine, but he was sober on this particular morning and he knew the risks of the job. He took a handkerchief out of his pocket and wiped his forehead. Then he took the blowtorch off his belt, leaned against the boiler so he could use both hands, and reached for his lighter. He realized his mistake too late. Combustible gases had escaped and hung in the air like gasoline vapors. As soon as the flint sparked, there was a flash, and chunks of metal went flying. Van crashed against the roof rafters and plummeted fifty feet to the cement floor, his body shattered and charred beyond recognition.

The wail of sirens was common in Covington as ambulances sped from the mill carrying workers to the hospital in Clifton Forge. For many of them, the last ride was to Cedar Hill Cemetery down by the Jackson River.

If town residents got used to the sirens, they had a harder time with the stink that emanated from the mill. It was pervasive and relentless. The air felt thick and sticky, as if a celestial chef were boiling up a vat of rotten cabbage just overhead. On the best days, when the wind blew toward West Virginia, the reek was tolerable. But when there was no breeze, the stench settled on the town like tarpaper, and breathing was a conscious effort.

My Aunt Hilda lived on Lexington Avenue, half a mile from the mill.

"How do you tolerate the smell?" I once asked her.

"Honey, that's the scent of money," she said. The paper mill kept the residents employed and the shops in business. Their lives depended on the mill.

Up Main Street, behind the courthouse and over the treetops, the towers of the mill belched their pong day and night, through Christmas and Fourth of July, marriages and deaths, celebrations and sorrows. Soot fell over the town and settled on the streets, the porches, the gardens, and the bed linens hanging on the clotheslines. By evening on summer days, children had dirt in their ears, between their toes and in the creases of their necks and elbows. When they blew their noses at night, black snot came out. Grime hung on the air like dark ghosts. The smell could not be escaped even in the local tavern, but alcohol dulled the senses enough to endure it.

In the midst of such industrial ugliness, the train that stopped at the Covington station carried, ironically, some of the world's most prominent and influential people. A few blocks from the station, the Intermont Hotel was once reputed to be the finest accommodation between Cincinnati and Washington. Wide verandas overlooked a two-acre lawn, landscaped with flowers and shrubs, that opened to views of the gentle Blue Ridge Mountains. Marble decorated the hallways, and the ceilings were painted with intricate designs in gold and heavenly blue.

When the hotel opened in May 1891, a banquet for the rich and famous was held in the chandeliered ballroom lined with heavy oak and mahogany. Guests came from New York, Washington, Cincinnati, and Chicago. The Intermont's hundred rooms filled up, and cots were set up in the halls for the overflow. An orchestra from Washington occupied the ballroom stage for dancing. Liquor ran freely, much of it supplied by mountain distillers, and the drink bill totaled $2,500. Author Gay Arritt reports that many of the partygoers were not able to navigate for a week.

At the close of the party, one of Covington's prominent citizens, not wishing to appear less affluent than the out-of-towners, yelled for his hired man to "bring around my coach and four." The fellow replied, "But boss, we don't have but one hoss." Miffed, the citizen whispered, "Well, bring it around and hitch it up."

The Intermont's guests were from distinguished families such as the J. Pierpont Morgans as well as lawyers, judges, politicians, and authors. To serve so many guests, a larger ballroom and more bedrooms were added. The room rates were $2.50 to $4 per day and $10 to $20 per week with special rates for those who stayed a month. But over time the number of guests dwindled, making it harder and harder to meet expenses, and finally the business was sold. The new owner commented that he had bought "a $15,000 white elephant and added a $20,000 tail," Arritt says. For a few months the owner turned the ballroom into a roller-skating rink. Then in 1913, broke and defeated, he gave up. After a glorious run, the hotel was torn down.

More often, dignitaries who got off the train in Covington were met by a sleek car whose driver swept them away from the foul stench of the paper mill and escorted them high into the mountains, depositing them at The Homestead. In the mid-eighteenth century, one of Washington's military commanders was granted 300 acres of land at Hot Springs, fifteen twisty mountain miles north of Covington. In the summer of 1834, the writer James Ewell Heath documented the journey over what he called "almost perpendicular ridges" with sharp switchbacks where, he says, at one point "you may look from your carriage window upon the traveller some fifty feet below, parallel with yourself, and, paradoxical as it may appear, proceeding in the same direction, although he is bound for the opposite end of the road."

The roads were so steep that my grandfather drove up in reverse, the strongest gear in his Model A Ford, honking his horn to warn oncoming autos that might swerve to the wrong side of the narrow road as they descended. I remember him saying that the turns were so sharp, "you can reach back and kiss your own ass."

Heath recognized the beauty of the area. "The deep vales and sun-tinged peaks seemed to be still slumbering in their original wildness . . . which had never before echoed but to the cry of the panther, or the war-whoop of the wandering Indian." He made note of "the numerous streams reflected in silvery sheets, as they wound through the broken country and hurried along to pour their waters into the bosom of the James [River]." A private distiller could not hope for better resources or privacy to practice his trade.

The temperature drops as you pass Falling Springs Falls where warm spring waters cascade over a cliff onto mossy rocks two hundred feet below. Near the top of the mountain, the trees open to a view of the Shenandoah Valley and the great Blue Ridge that runs south until "lost in the deeper azure of the evening sky, or hid by the dark and heavy clouds which bear the summer's storm," Heath says.

At Hot Springs, the imposing red brick mansion of The Homestead rises from a green field. Built in 1766 with brick from factories near Covington, the complex comprises indoor badminton and outdoor tennis courts, a golf course, skeet shooting, horse and hiking trails, and the healing waters and treatments of the spa. When Heath soaked in the waters, he felt "an almost immediate reduction of the pulse. Instances are known where the pulsations have been reduced from one hundred and twenty to eighty in the space of twenty-four hours." The reduction in blood pressure may have been aided by doses of the local liquor.

The Homestead enticed an impressive class of guests. Thomas Jefferson and James Madison stayed there. Thomas Edison built a power plant for the resort. Presidents Harrison, McKinley and Taft took the train from Washington to Covington and were met by limousines that drove them to The Homestead. Woodrow Wilson spent his honeymoon there. Calvin Coolidge and Herbert Hoover fished in the nearby streams. Roosevelt and Truman checked in, and Eisenhower, whose doctor advised him to exercise for his heart, played golf on the manicured course. Presidents Nixon, Johnson, Carter, Reagan, Bush and Clinton slept, ate, and—except for Carter—drank there as well.

Moonshining was both glamorous and smutty, and there was a romance surrounding its manufacture and its subversive character. I phoned and asked the manager what the resort did for liquor during Prohibition. He put me on hold. When the on-site historian picked up, she said, "There's a locker room in the back of the building. During Prohibition, guests brought their own liquor and secured it in lockers."

"What if they arrived emptyhanded?" I asked.

The Homestead's patrons were a demanding lot. After a pause, she said, "We had connections with backwoods operations." It appears that The Homestead supported the local economy in more ways than one.

One afternoon in the 1930s, a private rail car stopped in Covington. Whenever politicians and celebrities came through on their way to the Homestead, crowds of locals gathered at the station. That day my mother was among them. She remembers the arrival of a private car hooked to a passenger train. The Rockefellers, Woolworths and

Vanderbilts traveled in these types of first-class rail cars, and their arrival always caused a stir among Covington's citizens.

When the train rumbled in, cameras flashed, hats waved, and hands reached toward the moving cars. Men in dark jackets pushed the crowd back. The cars screeched to a stop and conductors hopped onto the platform. Behind them, people in business suits spilled out, a few men in uniform, and a woman struggling with a suitcase, all merging quickly into the throng.

From the private car men unloaded boxes. My mother heard bottles clink when the boxes were set in the trunk of a shiny black auto—wine and whiskey, she presumed. Prohibition had ended, and there was a war in Europe. It was a sure bet that there was no Virginia moonshine in those bottles. Anyone riding in an exclusive rail car could afford the best.

A woman stopped in the doorway, and for a second the crowd on the platform hushed. She wore a plain, tailored suit with a string of pearls at the neck, a classy black hat, dark hair coiled at the back of her head. A fox stole draped over her thin shoulders. Someone called out, "Duchess" and another, "Miss Simpson," and she waved a white gloved hand. Wallis Simpson was thin, and she stood straight, making her look taller. Lifting her head, she rose above the stink of the paper mill and the struggle of the average citizen to make ends meet. Behind her, a middle-aged man appeared. The Duke of Windsor was boyishly handsome and polished. He nodded toward the platform, and a hand reached up and helped the Duchess from the train. My mother, herself newly married, watched as the royals ducked into the sleek auto and were whisked up the mountain road toward The Homestead.

That day my mother had her closest brush with royalty. She would never ride in a fancy black auto and never taste expensive imported wines. She rarely drank at all except on special occasions when she might sip a terribly sweet potion, like a piña colada or a sloe gin fizz. Most of the time she was happy with a glass of homemade lemonade or iced tea. She was not pampered. Her family had coaxed a living from the land and the mills around it, and they had worked with dignity and pride. Two hundred years earlier, her ancestors had left their country by choice, unlike the Duke and Duchess who were no longer welcome in England and lived in voluntary exile between France and the United States.

With today's fast automobiles, one can drive from D.C. to Hot Springs in four hours, but until 1970, every dignitary who visited The Homestead resort went first through humble Covington, a town of contrasts and one whose history is flavored with moonshine.

Across a mountain ridge from Covington lies the hamlet of Buchanan. The town sits along Route 11 and was a major point on the Blue Ridge transportation corridor to the Chesapeake Bay via the James River, which passes through the town.

Buchanan was my father's childhood home and his father, Moody Pack Bryant, had a feed store on Main Street. Moody Pack sold corn meal, barley, yeast, and a sweet feed made with a mixture of grains flavored with molasses—a favorite of both livestock farmers and moonshiners. Before he discovered the lucrative market for farm supplies and whiskey ingredients, Moody Pack supported his family of twelve children by taking garden vegetables to town and trading them for buckshot so he could put meat on the dinner table. But there was real money to be made in distilling supplies. He was a man of discretion, and business was brisk. He took moonshiners' money and minded his own business.

In the post-Prohibition years, my Aunt Gladys and her husband opened a general store that carried essentials like milk, bread and ice cream. Out back in the garage she made dandelion wine, and I have a memory of her sipping a particularly potent vintage while she dealt hands of penny-ante poker as a tape recorder played a rerun of Sunday morning's service at the local Baptist church.

"Jesus drank wine," she said. "If it was good enough for him, it's good enough for me."

In the 1960s, a work crew was constructing the new Interstate 81 that runs parallel to Route 11. There were no hotels for the men to stay overnight, so local residents put them up for a reasonable fee. But what were the men to do in the evenings besides stare up at the black sky studded with silver sequins? Buchanan had no bars, and the nearest liquor store, twenty miles away in Roanoke, closed as the men were getting off work for the night.

My aunt was enterprising. She married four times, each husband richer than the previous one, and with the thirsty workers bunked in town, Gladys saw opportunity. She thought of setting up a still, but the process seemed too messy and complicated. So she did the next best thing. She drove to Roanoke and bought cheap whiskey in gallon bottles, brought it home and divided it into pint-size mason jars. Then she stashed the jars under the store's counter and whispered word around that her doors would be open late on weeknights so the workers could buy necessities. While highway construction was underway, Aunt Gladys made a tidy income. As for the tax, she figured she'd already paid the duty on the gallon, and it wasn't right to reimburse the government twice for the same liquid. The workers were happy, and Aunt Gladys stashed away a little extra money for a rainy day.

In small towns, people watch out for each other. They protect one another. Whiskey agents traveled the back roads and bought their lunches at country stores like the one my Aunt Gladys ran. She passed their sandwiches across the very counter under which she had stashed those jars of whiskey, and no one said a word.

■   ■   ■   ■   ■

The Homestead dining room offers a brown-sugar-brined chicken breast on its classic menu. Southerners traditionally sweeten their main dishes to entice appetite, and often they add a bit of liquor if it's available. When I was growing up, fried chicken was on the table at least once a week. My mother cut up a whole chicken, dredged it in flour and fried it in lard or shortening. When it came to the table, my brothers and I leaped first for the juicy dark meat, more delicious than the pale breasts which we left for our parents.

Here's an indulgent recipe for sweet chicken thighs with a heady whiskey sauce.

Peach Whiskey Chicken

Prep time: 5 minutes
Cook time: 2 hours
Ingredients:
12 chicken thighs (including bones and skin)
2 tablespoons olive oil
2 tablespoons butter
1 yellow onion, diced
1-1/2 cup whiskey
12-ounce jar barbecue sauce (or your own homemade)
1 jar peach preserves
½ cup water
2 tablespoons Worcestershire sauce
4 cloves garlic, peeled
3 green onions, sliced thin

Preparation:
Preheat oven to 300 degrees.
In a heavy ovenproof pot, heat oil and butter over medium-high heat. Add chicken thighs skin side down (4 at a time). Brown both sides. Remove to plate and repeat until all thighs are browned. Pour off half the fat and return pot to burner. Add onions and cook for 2 minutes. Add whiskey to deglaze the pan and reduce for a minute. Add barbecue sauce and entire jar of peach preserves. Put warm water into empty preserve jar and shake to get the last bits of jam from the sides. Add to pot. Add Worcestershire sauce and whole garlic cloves. Stir. Return chicken to the pot, skin side up, including juice that collected on the plate. Cover and put the pot into the hot oven. Cook 1-1/2 hours.
Serve pieces over mashed potatoes. Sprinkle green onions for garnish.
Yield: 6 servings.

Pine Cliff, Arcadia, Virginia (Family Photo)

Great Uncle Bures Paxton and compatiots at the still. (Family Photo)

Great-Grandfather John Henry and Annie Elizabeth Nida. (Family Photo)

Broad Run Tollhouse (Loudoun County VA archive)

Chapter 4 ~ Moonshining Women

She had got a kind of personal feeling about the machine she drove. It seemed beautifully alive to her. There was an exhilaration, a kind of half madness. Sometimes as she drove thus, every moment taking the chance of throwing her life away, she talked aloud to the machine. In a sense she loved it.
~ from the novel *Kit Brandon* by Sherwood Anderson

The German expression *Wenn schon denn schon* translates: "Anything worth doing is worth doing right." My mother had many characteristics of her German ancestors. She taught me the proper way to hang clothes on a line, fold a fitted sheet, and starch and iron a shirt wrinkleless. Her rose garden was weed free, and my brothers knew to mow the lawn in straight lines. The house was immaculately clean, rugs vacuumed, furniture polished. Sitting on an end table was a crystal dish of wrapped candies we children were not allowed to touch because they were for company. On the dining table, a glass bowl of fruit sat precisely center of a delicate cloth my mother had crocheted.

In our strict household, each of the four children had appointed tasks, and dinner was on the table at six o'clock. After dinner, my brothers cleared, my father washed, I dried, and my mother put away the dishes, inspecting their cleanliness before setting them in their proper cupboard places. But as fastidious as she was, she forgave a fumbled football fallen into the roses, she had a flirtatious way of tossing her hair, and she was the first to enjoy a prank or joke, head thrown back, laughing from her belly.

When I was growing up, iced tea was served with dinner—never wine and certainly not whiskey. Until I was ten or so, my father kept cans of beer in the refrigerator but when he grew too fond of it, my mother banned the brew from the house. She kept one bottle of

Canadian Club in the buffet, to be served only at Christmas to spike the eggnog. When my father drank, he did so the way men took their moonshine—outside, back of the garage, out of sight and hearing of women. In southern cultures sipping moonshine was not considered lady-like.

Moonshining conjures a wiry old mountain man, unkempt and snaggle-toothed, with a bushy beard. We usually think of white men as moonshiners, but Native Americans, African-Americans, and women did their share of brewing alcohol, too. Although distilling illegal liquor was widely thought to be a man's occupation, women were willing participants. In 1895, the American Whiskey Trail website says, over a hundred moonshiners were arrested in Huntington, West Virginia, many of them women. Men were harder to catch.

In 1870 Henry Berry Lowrie was the most hunted and feared man in North Carolina. It was illegal for a nonwhite to carry firearms, but Lowrie, a member of the Lumbee and Tuscarora Indian tribes, nevertheless carried a long-bladed knife, a double barrel shotgun, and five revolvers, according to UNC's Native American Tribal Studies. It was said that he had killed a couple men—one over stolen hogs and another over the treatment of women in his village of Scuffletown. A handsome ladies' man, Lowrie chose as his bride his sixteen-year-old cousin, the beautiful Rhoda Strong. On their wedding day, Lowrie was arrested and sent to prison, but he escaped by sawing his way through the bars with a file that most likely was sneaked to him by his new wife. Half Lumbee Indian and half Scot, Rhoda was admired by everyone in Robeson County. Her eyes, fierce as hot coals, penetrated under a mane of dark hair that fell in waves past her shoulders. While lying low from the prison posse, Lowrie fired up his still and made hooch, Rhoda by his side learning the process. When rich landowners tracked him down and accused him of robbing them to support the civil rights of his fellow natives, Lowrie disappeared and took ten thousand dollars of stolen money with him.

Even with a twenty-thousand-dollar reward for his capture, Lowrie slipped through the cracks, although it was claimed that he returned to see Rhoda under cover of night. Without her husband to depend on, Rhoda had nothing but her wits, her will, and her husband's still. Whether it was hunger or determination, she got the still going and sold jugs of Lowrie moonshine to eager buyers. Lawmen were frustrated with the elusive outlaw, and in 1897 they came onto the Lowrie property, shut down the still and charged Rhoda with retailing liquor without license. The judge fined her one hundred dollars and put her behind bars as bait for the bigger prize—her husband. When he didn't appear after thirty days, it was decided that Lowrie had to be dead to leave his wife incarcerated. Years later, after Rhoda's death, locals claimed they saw Lowrie coming out of the swamp to stand at her grave.

Since the beginning of the country, women have been involved with whiskey—or at least tolerated it. Martha Washington enjoyed the comforts and luxuries whiskey money provided her. Her husband's distillery business added to their already considerable wealth, and she did not object. During the Civil War, it was women who brought whiskey to the soldiers to keep their spirits up—and buoyed them in other ways as well.

Commanders turned a blind eye when women visited soldiers in the camps, with or without jars of whiskey. Union General Joseph Hooker not only had a tendency to tip the jug but also enjoyed the company of ladies. Hooker was a pretty man with sky blue eyes and a boyish face. He furnished his headquarters with prostitutes, and soldiers spoke of the general's war office as "a bar-room and a brothel," the RelicRecord site states. The liquor jugs never ran dry, and ladies of the evening were such frequent visitors to Hooker's Falmouth headquarters that they were known as "Hooker's girls." Later the term was shortened to "hookers," and the name stuck.

By the third year of the war, an estimated eight thousand women were working as prostitutes, most of them just outside military camps with easy access for soldiers. One soldier wrote to his wife, "It is said that one house in every ten is a bawdy house—it is a perfect Sodom." Venereal disease was epidemic and on occasion these working women, affectionately called "soiled doves," were told to pass the scourge on to enemy soldiers in a sort of germ warfare. During the war, prostitution was the only industry to cross enemy lines.

Smart women carried the rubber condoms that were being mass produced after Charles Goodyear patented vulcanized rubber in 1844. A rubber, as it came to be known, was thicker than condoms today and after it had served its purpose, the rubber was washed, preserved with petroleum jelly or oil, and stored in a wooden box until the next opportunity for use. Despite the fact that for three thousand years Egyptians had been using condoms made from sheep intestines, George Bernard Shaw declared that Goodyear's rubber was "the greatest invention of the nineteenth century," author Thomas Lowry says.

Rubbers not only thwarted the spread of disease but also helped prevent pregnancy. If a rubber wasn't available, a woman might press a small vinegar-soaked sponge into her vagina before intercourse, or she would use a rubber cervical cap called a "womb veil." In a pinch, if a man paid with a silver dollar, she inserted the coin to block the cervix. But if a soiled dove's efforts failed and she found herself with child, she hid the bump under thick skirts and tied an apron high over her belly, concealing the pregnancy for as long as she could. She had a living to earn, after all.

Other than prostitution and selling moonshine, there were not many ways for a single woman to support herself in lean times. Rather than arrest so many ladies of the evening, legislators decided to legalize the profession. Each prostitute had to obtain a license, and the penalty for working without a license was a month in jail. They also had to submit to weekly medical examinations and pay a tax of fifty cents every week to support a hospital for invalids, measures that not only protected and legitimized the profession but turned sin into charity.

Women may have slept with men, but they didn't necessarily drink with them. Unlike bars and speakeasies of big cities, social drinking didn't exist in the mountains of Appalachia. Men either abstained or privately drank themselves into a stupor. A hunting or fishing trip was an excuse to down a few swigs hidden by a screen of woods, and the hunters did not return home until they sobered up. If the imbibing occurred on a Saturday, a man had better be able to button up a high collar for church on Sunday, no matter how hung over he was. In the mountains, drinking whiskey in the open was frowned upon, but if a man were going to drink, he might as well get drunk. For women, the conventions were different.

A while ago I was a guest at a Kentucky garden party. From the stone patio, a meadow rolled down to the Ohio River where a hundred fifty years ago steamboats lazed along, smoke drifting from their stacks. On the covered porch, a fiddler and a guitarist played sprightly tunes. When they took a break, the guitarist picked up the mason jar at her feet and took a sip.

"What's she drinking?" I asked the host.

"Moonshine," the host said.

I didn't ask where the moonshine came from—it was taken for granted that everyone had a jar of moonshine hidden in a kitchen cabinet, and entertainers were offered a jar to help them find their groove. I preferred to visit the bartender, who poured expensive whiskey from bottles for which the host had paid the appropriate federal tax.

In the past, men perched on sawhorses or overturned buckets behind the barn to have a drink. When women drank, it was in groups with other females around an activity like a game of gin rummy. Another guest at the garden party told me of attending a quilting bee where she was working on a quilt with five other women. They had stitched the blocks of fabric together, fitted the batting, and attached the backing. The quilt was on its frame, and the women gathered to sew the scrolling design that holds the quilt layers together. They'd just begun when the man of the house came home. He was deputy sheriff of the county and had returned from busting up a moonshiner's still. The offender was sent off to prison, and the sheriff confiscated a gallon jar of the moonshine. He presented the jar to his wife, who poured each of her friends a tumbler of the potent juice. The women sipped while they sewed, getting happier with each stitch. The more they drank, the lovelier their designs grew, the thread vines curling and whirling gracefully over the fabric. As it got late, the women agreed to meet the following week to finish the quilt and gave each other cheery hugs before leaving. When they reconvened, they found the quilting rack empty. The unfinished quilt had vanished. The women scoured the house, but no quilt. Finally, someone spotted a bundle tucked into the rafters of the kitchen and the package was retrieved. When they unwrapped the bundle, they found not the beautiful quilt they had labored over earlier, but a wretched mess with uneven stitches meandering in haphazard directions. No one remembered stashing the quilt into the lofty hiding place, and no one took the blame for the sloppy stitching. But patiently (and soberly) they pulled out the misbehaving threads and started again, this time without the enhancement of moonshine.

If you give ten women each a bag of the same scraps of cloth, they will sew ten different quilts. We are of every type—smart, ignorant, profane, God-fearing, faithful, lazy, hardworking, literary and illiterate. What makes women of Appalachia unique is that they have always loved their hill country. No matter how poor they are, when a stranger comes to the door, he is invited in to eat, drink, and sit a spell. If he needs a bed for the night, one is provided with a hearty breakfast in the morning.

One of my earliest memories is meeting my great-grandmother Annie Elizabeth Paxton Nida on a family visit to the Shenandoah Valley. My mother had taken me to have dinner, which was served just past noon, at her Aunt Emma's property "up on Potts Creek," as my mother said, where a stream gurgled clear and sparkling beside her house. "The little houses," Anderson wrote, "usually very small, tucked away on some side road, very narrow, winding and stony, almost always the house standing by a mountain stream." Building by a stream was preferable to digging a well, and the running water was useful for cooking and washing as well as for operating a still.

At Aunt Emma's house, four-by-four pine columns supported the porch, which ran the length of the house. Next to the door a basket filled with clothespins dangled from a rusty nail, ready for the washing to be hung out to dry. In the living room, the walls were papered with a pattern of white daisies. An iron bucket, bootjacks, and a red lantern sat beside the brick fireplace. The wood floor was painted green. In the kitchen, the linoleum bubbled in a continuous ripple from the back door to the dining room where a maple table was adorned with a doily that looked hand crocheted.

Aunt Emma greeted us with fleshy hugs. She was huge from years of eating food fried in pork grease. My mother and I helped carry dishes to the picnic table set in the front yard. Emma had laid out a generous spread—meatloaf brown as hill loam, mashed potatoes and gravy, melt-in-your-mouth green beans slow cooked with a slab of fatback, homemade biscuits, pickled beets, and thick slices of tomato and cantaloupe from the garden. On the wide porch, Annie Elizabeth sat on a wooden rocker, her white hair tied in a loose knot atop her head, the same way she wore it in the old pictures on my wall when her hair was brown. She was thin, a woman used to farm work, and had a pretty face even though lined with age. When she saw me, she sprang from her chair and came toward me, reaching down for my four-year-old self with outstretched arms. "Let me get my arms around you," she said. In my memory, her white dress came to her ankles and although she looked like a mature angel, I was terrified of her. I ran to my mother, who took me up, but I stole glimpses of my great-grandmother throughout the dinner. She must have been eighty then. Each time our eyes met, she smiled and the wrinkles fell from her face. I got over my fright and came to realize that she simply loved children. I wish now I could talk with her and have her tell me what life was like for her in Boiling Spring.

After Aunt Emma offered grace, we sat down to eat al fresco, although no one would have used that term. The dinner was generous and tasty. If there was a jug of moonshine sitting around, it was kept hidden from me. I think back to Annie Elizabeth, her poise and acceptance of my mother and me who had become outsiders when my father relocated the family to northern Virginia before I was born. Making liquor did not mean my people were slothful or dangerous or immoral. There was a time and place for everything, and that day at Aunt Emma's was a time for celebrating our kinship.

When Anderson set up house in the mountains of Virginia in 1925, he described citizens like my Blue Ridge relatives who stuck "tight to their barren hills like fleas on a dog. Little houses tucked away on some side road. . . , a cow and a barn right close up against the road. Every man with a bottle of moon whisky in his hip pocket ...," reports author Charles D. Thompson in his book *Spirits of Just Men*. With poverty forcing a bare bones existence, moonshine was the main cash crop for many Appalachia dwellers, and women not only tolerated the work at the stills but were involved in it.

When it comes to their liquor, Appalachians feel entitled to drink what they've produced from the corn and rye grown in their own fields using stills forged with their own hands. For many of them, putting a tax on corn liquor was like taxing the corn itself, and they were not going to stand for it, even if it meant serving a jail sentence. If the women spied alcohol and tobacco tax agents across a field, they "called the cows" by hollering out, "Come, Boss. Coooommmme BAAAAASSS!" A "whoop" or a honking horn carries across a field, and a revenuer might have thought a woman was rounding up the herd for milking rather than alerting their fellows of the presence of an intruder.

Anderson wrote in a 1934 issue of *Liberty Magazine* that Franklin County "fairly dripped illicit liquor," Thompson says. It's true that just a short drive down the valley from Boiling Spring, Franklin County has long been a major source of moonshine income. For decades, thousands of jars of the precious liquid have been transported to buyers in northern cities. During the dry period, women were recruited to run moonshine in gallon jars painted white. If a woman was stopped, she told the federal officer she was delivering milk from the family dairy farm.

Most of the drivers during Prohibition were men like Junior Johnson, whose parents operated what was reputed to be the largest copper still in North Carolina. Junior was eight years old when he learned to drive and was making liquor deliveries by the time he was fourteen, executing white-knuckle maneuvers to outsmart the law. Junior's "bootleg turn" was copied by other drivers who tried the 180-degree spin by slamming into second gear and jerking the steering wheel to the left, biographer Kerry Burns writes. On night runs, Junior hoodwinked the police with his lead foot and daredevil tactics.

But there were no gender restrictions on the tricks of driving fast. Willie Carter Sharpe was making her own bootleg turns from Franklin County every night to outrun the feds. Willie may not have earned the notoriety of Junior Johnson, but she did earn the title, "the queen of Roanoke rum runners."

Anderson thinly disguises Willie Carter Sharpe in his novel *Kit Brandon* as "a woman of twenty-five. She had bought a cheap model of a dress of the latest New York style. Her lips and cheeks were painted but she still had a snuff stick protruding from a corner of her mouth." When Anderson interviewed her, she wanted to talk in his car and insisted on doing the driving. "I think better when I'm driving a car," Kit Brandon said. As she drove, she began to talk. "Everyone wants to get their story told," Anderson said, "so the terrible isolation of their lives can break."

Born Willie May Collins on a farm in Floyd County, Virginia, Willie never saw a town until she was fifteen. She grew into a healthy, fine-looking woman with dark hair like her father's. In her twenties, she was not thought to be beautiful but was the kind of woman men admired rather than desired. Solidly built, she stood five feet five and weighed 157 pounds. Anything but dainty and feminine, she liked a smoke and a drink after work with her boots up on a table and would spit in your eye if you called her a lady.

One afternoon in 1920, Floyd Carter, the son of bootleg baron John Carter, walked into the dime store where Willie May Collins was working. Most people avoided the Carters, who had amassed a fortune in the liquor business and were known to be dangerous if you crossed them. But Willie was not cowed. She looked Floyd straight in the eye the way she did any other customer. He liked her spunk and asked her out on a date. She agreed on the condition that he let her drive his fancy convertible. Floyd was either smitten or figured she couldn't do much harm, and he relinquished the wheel to her. Growing up on the farm, Willie had learned the nuances of machinery, and to say that she could handle a car was an understatement. Floyd held onto his hat as Willie sped up country roads and over mountain passes, dust billowing up behind them. When finally she brought the car to a stop and switched off the engine, Floyd asked to see her again.

Floyd had never met a woman as audacious as Willie. After a brief courtship, he popped the question. Willie considered her options. Growing up poor and barefoot on her family's country property, she had done the work of a man until the age of sixteen. Floyd could give her things she'd only dreamed of. She would not be deprived again.

Willie took immediately to the bootleg business and talked Floyd's father into letting her drive for him. It never felt to her like breaking the law—she hadn't made the hooch and she wasn't selling it. If she was speeding, the law would have to catch her, and catching Willie Carter behind the wheel of a fast car was no easy task. By the time John Carter had her making runs every night, she was driving for the sheer ecstasy of it. Willie estimated that between 1926 and 1931, she had run 220,000 gallons of illicit whiskey from Franklin County as far north as New York, writes T. Keister Greer in *The Great Moonshine Conspiracy Trial of 1935.*

When Carter saw how cleverly she could work a vehicle, he assigned Willie the job of pilot—the driver of a decoy car that lured police cruisers into a high-speed chase, leaving the roads empty for convoys of illegal liquor to be delivered across the county line. Willie was the middleman—middle woman—having an exhilarating time behind the wheel of a quick machine.

A bootleg runner needed to have a faster car than the law, so they spent hours on their autos. They fitted vehicles with bright rear-facing lights to blind pursuing revenuers and switched license plates to confuse the feds. They muscled up engines by adding three two-barrel carburetors to a Cadillac motor installed in a Ford body. The carburetors had to be shortened in order to close the hood of the car. A supercharger rammed additional air into the cylinders, and some vehicles had as many as fifteen forward gears. Mechanics added a sixteen-gallon fuel tank and extra suspension springs to hold the vehicle level even when carrying a full load of whiskey. It was not unusual to see an unloaded auto with its hind end reaching for the sky. With a trunk stacked full, including a hidden compartment under the trunk bed, a load of liquor could weigh over a thousand pounds. If you heard the sound of a big engine, you made sure to get out of the road pronto.

Some runners used delivery vans or pickups with a tarp over the hooch and a load of mulch or topsoil piled on the tarp to look like a routine farm delivery. Willie's preference was a car, a more maneuverable conveyance than a truck. With the flick of a special switch, she could turn off her taillights, making her harder to spot from behind. When revenuers shot at her tires, she took to dark country roads and lost them on deadly curves and steep ascents. She came alive when she drove, adrenaline rushing through her veins, every nerve alert.

Willie could earn fifty dollars a night driving through town streets at speeds of seventy-five miles per hour, according to Thompson. With the money she bought silk suits and shoes of Italian leather, things she had never dreamed of owning before bootleg driving. It was said that she had diamonds set in her teeth. Where she once had nothing, now nothing was too good for her. Money bought her respectability—as long as she could outrun the law.

One night in 1931 as Willie was driving pilot, the car's brakes failed. Federal agents were tailing her, and she careened down a side street to lose them. Doubling back, she whirled into an intersection and, not able to stop, rammed the side of the agents' car. She crawled from the wreck, her arms sliced and bleeding. The men were cut up pretty badly, too. Any runner worth his salt would have taken to the woods, but Willie had a soft spot. She stayed and helped the agents out of their banged up vehicle. There was no liquor in her car, but the agents put her under arrest for reckless driving. "Reckless? Willie protested. "Why, it was inspired!" Inspired or not, a judge sent her to federal prison for three years, writes Anderson.

While she was behind bars, Willie had visitors, many of them blue-blood women dolled up in expensive dresses. She had become a sort of romantic muse, the wild spirit other women dreamed of being but didn't have the gumption for. One young woman asked if she could ride with Willie when she got out of jail. The lady wanted the adventure of a high-speed chase, making complex maneuvers, getting away with lawlessness. Outrunning cops had become the new extreme sport. Willie told the woman she was finished with driving, but within a week of her release, she was running moonshine again. The speed—and the money—were addicting.

Between 1930 and 1935, moonshiners in Franklin County were the recipients of thirty-seven tons of yeast, seventeen thousand tons of sugar, and thousands of tons of malt, meal and other materials used in making whiskey, along with a million five-gallon cans made specifically for liquor, writes Thompson. As the illegal distilling business picked up, so did federal investigations. In 1935 a federal grand jury indicted thirty-four people for conspiracy to defraud the federal government of tax money. Those indicted included a Franklin County sheriff and several of his deputies, a state prohibition officer, a former House of Delegates member, the Franklin County Commonwealth's Attorney, and Willie Carter Sharpe. By then she had divorced Floyd Carter and moved in with a bootlegger named Charlie Sharpe. Although they never officially married, she added his name to hers. The trial lasted forty-nine days, and 176 witnesses were called to the stand, Greer reports.

Witnesses admitted to moving at least a million gallons of whiskey, and it was estimated that one hundred million gallons of moonshine were transported out of the county each year. The prosecution estimated that the conspirators had defrauded the federal government of five and a half million dollars in whiskey excise taxes and argued that a conspiracy to avoid taxes was akin to robbing the government treasury, thereby robbing people served by that government. But one witness countered, "Anyone would tell you you cannot legislate morality, and you certainly can't stop people from drinking," Greer writes.

Willie was witness number 154. Wearing a white tailored dress with brown ruffled sleeves, a white hat and shoes to match, and a cameo brooch pinned to the front of her collar, she looked to be the picture of moral uprightness.

Her fellow bootleggers defended her. One testified: "The illegal liquor trade is worth tens of billions . . . , and it's not Willie Carter Sharpe who's in charge. It's gangsters. Organized crime has a stranglehold stretching across the country." He listed half a dozen mobsters in major cities, including Chicago's Al Capone, whom he called "the most notorious gangster of all." Capone, he said, earned over a hundred dollars a minute from illegal alcohol.

The testimony was convincing. Obviously there were larger fish to fry, and Willie was set free to take to the road again.

Willie had paid her dues with jail time and court testimony. She gave up running moonshine and left Franklin County to live out her life in anonymity. But in the mountains of Virginia, Willie Carter Sharpe and her lawless driving are legend.

Not all women tolerated distilling substances—illegal or otherwise. Forty-five years before Prohibition, women gathered in Cleveland to form the Woman's Christian Temperance Union. Their goal was to keep men away from alcohol that made them mean and violent and get them back to work so they could feed their families. Groups of women led by Frances Willard, Anna Gordon, and Ella Boole lobbied legislators to dry up America in order to protect themselves and their children, the primary victims of alcohol abuse. When the Eighteenth Amendment passed, it appeared that alcohol would be banned forever. According to American Whiskey Trail site, Senator Morris Shepard, who co-wrote the Amendment, said, "There is as much chance of repealing the Eighteenth Amendment as there is for a humming-bird to fly to the planet Mars with the Washington Monument tied to its tail." Shepard was proven wrong, of course, but not even a constitutional amendment was going to stop citizens from enjoying their liquor.

In Burlington, Vermont, near where I now live, a whiskey bar offers 130 varieties of distilled liquors. Among them is Laphroaig from a Scottish distillery. In the 1930s Laphroaig was run by a young woman named Bessie Williamson, who took to making liquor as if it ran in her veins. When I first tasted the Laphroaig, I found the whiskey too smoky for my palate, but with patience the flavor can be appreciated. During Prohibition, Williamson came to America to promote her malt whiskey, selling it as a "medicinal spirit." As with medicinal marijuana, whiskey could be obtained with a prescription from a doctor, and even now old timers refer to strong drink as their "medicine." After Prohibition ended, Williamson visited the Chicago World's Fair and the New York Trade Fair as the Scotch Whisky Association's international ambassador.

Although Bessie Williamson was the most famous female distiller in Scotland, she was not the only one. A rummage through the distillery lists in the Hume & Moss volume, *The Making of Scotch Whisky*, finds well over twenty women connected with distilleries.

In the U.S., women were having a change of heart. They were fed up with the muscling of organized crime and the ridiculous amounts of money being amassed by gangsters, and they objected to government interfering with their private lives. As early as 1922, a group of New York women formed the Molly Pitcher Club with the aim of ending prohibition. They took the name from the Revolutionary War heroine who got women to carry water to men on the battlefield. When her husband was wounded, Molly took up his gun and fought the British herself. The members of the New York club became known as "Molly Pitchers," and their mission was to prevent "any tendency on the part of our National Government to interfere with the personal habits of the American people except those habits which may be designated as criminal." Drinking alcohol was a personal choice, they said, and making spirits for one's own consumption should not be considered unlawful.

The Association Against the Prohibition Amendment (AAPA) estimated that eleven billion dollars was lost in federal liquor tax revenue between 1920 and 1930, but three hundred million dollars had been spent on prohibition enforcement. With the country already struggling with economic depression and high unemployment, the repeal of the Eighteenth Amendment was crucial. John D. Rockefeller and the du Pont brothers, all highly influential in business and politics, supported repeal.

When women earned the right to vote, they added their voices to the voting polls. Pauline Sabin, a wealthy and prominent New York socialite, saw the hypocrisy of politicians who supported Prohibition but managed to acquire bottles of illegal whiskey for their private use. If they were breaking the law and gangsters were killing each other for the sake of unlawful liquor, what message was trickling down to the nation's children? When in 1929 Sabin founded the Women's Organization for National Prohibition Reform (WONPR), Republicans sneered and called them a "wine-drinking society of women." Four years later, when the repeal was passed by a vote of three to one, the organization's membership ballooned to a million and a half with branches in forty-one states. Sabin appeared on the cover of *Time* magazine, even though she received letters like the one that swore, "Every evening I get down on my knees and pray to God to damn your soul."

Franklin Delano Roosevelt ran for president and as part of his platform promised to repeal Prohibition. When the state conventions ratified the Twenty-First Amendment, it was the first and only time in United States history that a Constitutional amendment was overturned. Alcohol was once again legal, thanks to the efforts of strong, outspoken women. But even after Prohibition ended, the moonshine industry in Virginia's Blue Ridge continued to flourish. Legalizing liquor gave the government the opportunity to tax it once again, and southerners still rankled at giving up their hard-earned money to an administration run by Yankees. Moonshiners like those in Franklin County continued to get rich by running hooch, and local history reports that a few bootleggers from the area held onto tens of thousands of dollars in the midst of the Great Depression.

My mother remembers riding to the bank with her father when she was fourteen. With the Depression gripping him and his neighbors, he planned to withdraw his life's savings and keep it in a safe place until things turned around. He told her to wait in the car while he conducted business inside. In less than an hour he returned, his face pale. He sat in the driver's seat and gripped the steering wheel. His money—every cent he had saved—had evaporated. He put his forehead against his hands and wept. It was the only time my mother saw her father cry.

If ever my grandfather were tempted to join the liquor trade, it was that day during the Depression. Instead, he picked himself up and went on. He had a job at the mill, and he'd get through the hard times somehow. He had a garden and he had pigs and chickens. If he wanted a shot of whiskey—and at that moment he could have used one—there were plenty of stills nearby to accommodate him. He did not need to operate his own—he had far too much to do to keep his family fed.

■ ■ ■ ■ ■

Northerners balk at adding brown sugar and honey to sweet potatoes, a root vegetable already naturally saccharine, but for southerners, the addition of syrup to anything makes it that much more delectable. Sprinkle in a little moonshine and you have a dish that is heaven on earth. Here is a recipe for sweet potatoes with an intoxicating additive.

Honey and Whiskey Candied Sweet Potatoes

Prep time: 30 minutes
Cook time: 1 hour

Ingredients:
1/4 cup (1/2 stick) unsalted butter
1/4 cup light-flavored honey such as wildflower, orange blossom, or clover
2 tablespoons whiskey (or more, to taste)
2 tablespoons (packed) dark brown sugar
3 pounds sweet potatoes (or yams), peeled and halved or quartered
3/4 teaspoon salt
3/4 teaspoon freshly ground black pepper

Preparation:
Preheat oven to 375°F.
Butter a 2-quart casserole dish.
In small saucepan over moderately high heat, combine butter, honey, whiskey, and sugar. Bring to simmer, whisking until butter and sugar are melted, then reduce heat to moderately low and simmer, uncovered, 10 minutes.
In large bowl, toss potatoes with butter mixture, salt, and pepper. Transfer to prepared dish and bake until tender and glazed, about 45 minutes. Serve warm.
Yield: 8 to 10 servings

Chapter 5—Temperance Spirits

Now Daddy ran the whiskey in a big black Dodge
Bought it at an auction at the Mason's Lodge
Johnson County Sheriff painted on the side
Just shot a coat of primer then he looked inside—
Well him and my uncle tore that engine down
I still remember that rumblin' sound.
~ Steve Earle, from the song "Copperhead Road"

Between minor disasters like a fire in the movie theater projection booth and the Jackson overflowing onto River Street every spring, a mountain town like Covington gnaws on itself for amusement. My mother, left a widow with two young boys, got a job at the mill driving a forklift and stacking heavy spools of paper into giant towers. Her pitiful salary met the rent on an apartment and paid a housekeeper to take care of the boys while she was at work. The community gave her both sympathy and criticism—a woman should be home with her children, not doing a man's job. She met a sailor when he was home on leave from the Navy and married him quickly. He was scheduled to be shipped to the Pacific, and there was no time to waste. When he returned from his tour of duty, he was stationed in Washington, D.C., and took the train to Covington on weekends. The separation wore on them both, and when my mother found herself pregnant, it was time for a new arrangement.

To be with my father, my mother uprooted her sons and moved to Arlington, Virginia, just yards from the Washington border. There was much she missed about Covington—spring cowslip and dog violet, summer gardens, and the friendly old Blue Ridge. The Shenandoah Valley was the only home she had known, but she was young and strong and, like her German ancestors, she would adapt.

My mother had known most of the African American residents of Covington who lived on the side of Fore Mountain, but she wasn't expecting to be in a racial minority in Washington. The nation's capital had declared emancipation months before Abe Lincoln issued his proclamation, and freed slaves flocked to the urban area. By 1900, Washington had the largest percentage of blacks of any city in the country and by midcentury greater than half the population was African American, says Marya Annette McQuirter on the website Cultural Tourism D.C. In 1975, when I was a graduate student at George Washington University, blacks numbered above 70% of Washington's citizens.

In the previous century, African Americans struggled to find ways to support themselves in an urban environment. For women, landing a paying job in the legal job market was nearly impossible. In desperation, many black women turned to bootlegging or numbers running, an illegal lottery masterminded by organized crime. Risking arrest was better than homelessness or starvation, and there was glamour in hanging out in the nighttime world of leisure and pleasure.

Odessa Marie Madre's parents moved to Washington in the 1920s and became well-to-do in the barber and pool hall businesses. They had hopes that their daughter would go into teaching. Instead, Odessa chose to operate in the underground economy, says Sharon Harley in her book *Sister Circle*. Madre was no beauty, and her dark skin kept her from social and business circles where her lighter complexioned friends found success. But what she lacked in looks she made up for in brains and bravado. Her parents had given her a parcel of valuable real estate, and in the 1930s she sold it and bought two houses in "Cowtown," now the Adams Morgan area of the District. She lived in one house and in the other she opened a "jill joint" selling bootleg liquor, drugs and sex. Her club enticed celebrities like Count Basie and boxer Joe Lewis. She cut her cocaine with sugar and business prospered. For forty years Madre operated six houses of prostitution employing twenty women, two illegal saloons, and a bookmaking enterprise at 16th and U Streets in the city's northwest section. Her one legitimate business, Club Madre, was a chic nightspot where Madre appeared dressed in furs and diamonds followed by light-skinned black and Asian women for hire by the evening. By 1950, when her annual net income was said to be around a hundred thousand dollars, Madre was known as the queen of Washington's underworld.

While Madre was splashing whiskey into patrons' glasses, D.C. boy Bill France was skipping school and driving his father's Model T Ford into the Maryland suburbs. Laurel had a mile and a half oval board track, a steeply sloped run made of wood where France pushed the old auto for all she was worth. He dreamed of going to Daytona Beach where land speed records had been set on tracks of packed beach sand, making treacherous turns over sandy ruts, records the website The Father of NASCAR. Many of the Laurel drivers hauled moonshine at night, honing their skills on twisting mountain roads and taking the same vehicle to the track the next day. The heavier vehicles mired down in the muck while lighter cars grabbed the prizes. Once a moonshine vehicle had delivered its haul, it practically skimmed over the sand. Speed was like a drug, and the illegal transports became the darlings of the legal racing world. Spectators paid to live the thrill vicariously. Entering a stockcar race required nerve, will, and a bit of foolhardiness, but the drivers who took their chances and won races became legends.

Young Bill France was in love with automobiles. During the Depression, his pockets empty, he migrated to Daytona. By 1947 he had made money winning races and became a recognized name in drag racing. He began promoting auto racing as a sport and a year later Big Bill, as he came to be called, founded the National Association for Stock Car Auto Racing. NASCAR would become America's biggest spectator sport, thanks in no small part to moonshiners and their modified engines.

France was getting rich in Daytona, yet outside the nation's capital times were hard. Yards were tilled for gardens and hunters took wild game to an open-air market in Alexandria and sold it, but the average man had a tough time providing for his family. The creeks and streams in the area ran with clear water, and the woods afforded plenty of places to hide a still. Making moonshine became a way of life.

Distillers vented the smoke through the chimneys of their homes and hid mason jars of whiskey under their beds, always keeping an eye out for federal agents. In Northern Virginia, Buck Howard, a Lorton moonshine distiller, spied two agents coming through the woods and ran home, leaving his coat behind. The agents recognized the coat and confronted Howard with it. Luckily, he had an identical coat in his closet. Howard denied the guilty garment was his and produced the second coat. The feds were fooled again and let him go free, writes author Eugene Scheel of Loudoun County.

A federal agent destroyed another Lorton still and then crossed the road to the home of one Mr. Hicks to ask for a drink of water from his well. "I just raided your still across the road," the agent said, ready to make an arrest. "Not my still," Mr. Hicks replied. Indeed the still did not belong to Mr. Hicks because his was hidden in his shed near the very well where the agent was quenching his thirst.

A stonemason named Earl Batt built a still on Tenfoot Island in the middle of the Potomac River ten miles east of Washington in Loudoun County, Maryland. Batt bought his coarse brown sugar at a country store whose shopkeeper always kept a supply of sugar and yeast on hand. To throw inquisitive revenuers off his trail, the shopkeeper told them that the sugar went to confectionary stores. Batt ran his moonshine by powerboat to the Virginia shore and sold it for three dollars for a half-gallon jar, a fair price in the 1930s. Maryland officials didn't bother with him, since he was selling to Virginians, but when Old Dominion authorities came after him, Batt dismantled the still, stowed it in the powerboat and threw a cover over the boat until the coast was clear, Scheel writes. Locals who remember Batt's product say he was the mainstay for the moonshine supply.

A Virginia farmer in Sterling, an hour outside the District, rented a section of his property to vegetable growers. When he went down to the cow barn one morning, he looked across the field at apparatus that hadn't been there the day before. He recognized the equipment—a still.

The farmer didn't want to cause trouble, but he'd have to speak to the renters. The next morning when he went to the barn, the still was gone. Later when he was walking at the field's edge, he found an unfamiliar trail into the woods. He followed the path and found the same still. A week later, the operation was broken down and set up in another clearing in the woods. Some days there was no trace of the illegal contraption, and then suddenly he'd come upon it as if he'd conjured the operation himself. Clever, these renters, keeping the revenuers guessing and making them work for their money.

When I grew up in Northern Virginia just off Leesburg Pike, Washington was exactly six miles from our house. The legal age for alcohol in Virginia at that time was twenty-one, but just over the Key Bridge in Georgetown, eighteen-year-olds could consume beer and liquor. I often borrowed my father's VW and kept an eye on the mileage because I had told him I was just going to a friend's house a couple miles away. Frugality stuck with him from the Depression years, and in a notebook he stashed in the glove compartment he recorded miles driven and miles per gallon. I drove the twelve miles round trip to Georgetown and then stopped at a suburban mall parking lot, put the car in reverse, and maneuvered large circles—backwards—until I'd run off five or six miles, adding a dribble of gas to the tank to try to even things out. One morning my father raised an eyebrow and mentioned that he seemed to be getting exceptionally good gas mileage in the Beetle.

In earlier years, drivers on Leesburg Pike were required to stop at a tollhouse to pay a fee for crossing a bridge over Broad Run, a tributary of the Potomac River. Built in the late eighteenth century, the Broad Run Tollhouse is a stalwart stone structure with a slate roof and sturdy chimneys. A stone wall guards against trespassers. The original wooden bridge washed away in a flood and was replaced by a marvel of modern nineteenth century engineering with sandstone toted from a quarry in Virginia's Blue Ridge Mountains and hand chiseled into blocks. In its earliest days, tolls were determined by the vehicle—a shilling for a coach or a loaded wagon, eight pence for a cart. During Prohibition, the crossing fee was waived, but two distillers named Holsinger and Jenkins set up shop in the tollhouse. Word spread, and the tollhouse was back in business. Once again drivers halted at the stone building, this time making a transaction—two bucks for a pint of moonshine.

While they waited for customers, Holsinger and Jenkins sampled their own product. One night they argued over whose whiskey was better, who was attracting the most customers, or who was making more money. The quarrel grew more and more heated until Holsinger pulled a .22 and fired on Jenkins at close range, killing him. After Jenkins's death, the tollhouse was locked shut and customers had to find another source for their drinking pleasure, writes Scheel.

Stills were often guarded with pistols and shotguns. These were rugged times, and to a moonshiner the term "taking the law into your own hands" has always been a grassroots statute that permits one to act unlawfully in the name of personal justice. It was, they were convinced, a matter of individual rights.

Federal agents have been shot dead on raids in northern Virginia and Maryland, and in many cases no arrests were made. In one case, Jess Tomblin, a distiller of corn whiskey and apple brandy, sold so much of his product to the locals that wives of the drunken husbands reported the distiller to the local judge. The judge alerted Tomblin to stash all but a few jugs and then sent the sheriff to raid Tomblin's still. At his hearing, the judge slapped Tomblin's wrist, fined him ten bucks, and for the next decade continued to patronize Tomblin's business himself, Scheel says.

People from all walks of life in Northern Virginia and the Maryland suburbs colluded in the making and drinking of liquor—from presidents to dirt-poor farmers, from federal agents to clueless teenage girls. They sold sips of their liquor from straws slipped into Mason jars they had hidden in their coat pockets. Moonshiners' wives handed out samples from their kitchens to entice buyers and gave gallon jars of moonshine as wedding presents. When a distiller was arrested, patrons bought up the inventory. Making and distributing illegal liquor was an ingrained cultural trait.

At Lincoln, a D.C. restaurant, for ten bucks you'll be served Honest Abe's Moonshine, a cocktail consisting of a brand of white whiskey (aged for exactly seventy-two hours) with ginger and lemon. The café initiated the Mason Jar Program wherein each month they feature an imbibement that holds what the eatery calls "the spirit and history of the American cocktail." In 1833 Abe Lincoln himself was given a license to sell liquor in Illinois and opened and operated several taverns. He entered politics when the anti-alcohol movement was gaining strength and although he was an outspoken abolitionist, he straddled the fence on the issue of outlawing alcohol. I don't imagine he'd have objected to having a modern pub named after him.

America's leaders had differing views regarding the imbibing of intoxicating beverages. John Adams started drinking at age fifteen when he entered Harvard and regularly drank beer for breakfast. Presidents van Buren, Buchanan, Grant, Arthur, and Cleveland were notorious boozers. McKinley liked a whiskey before retiring at night. Benjamin Harrison reportedly said he would have been happier with a $2,000-a-year pension, a barrel of hard cider, and a log cabin to live in rather than serving as the 23rd president, writes author Sarah Jacobs.

Woodrow Wilson, under whose presidency the Volstead Act went into effect enforcing the Eighteenth Amendment, had a wine cellar in his house and enjoyed a glass of scotch in the evenings. President Harding kept the White House well stocked with bootleg liquor even though he had voted for Prohibition when he was in the Senate. Herbert Hoover opposed the Volstead Act but after working at the Commerce Department, he often stopped off for a cocktail at the Belgian Embassy, technically located on foreign land, giving the embassy immunity from Prohibition laws. Hoover grumbled that Prohibition's only accomplishment was forcing him to use up the impressive collection of bottles in his wine cellar.

Franklin Roosevelt liked fancy picnics in the country. My brother Don's father-in-law, Montford Snyder, was Roosevelt's chauffeur and told Don that on occasion he took out the back seat of the President's car and placed it on the ground for his dining comfort and that of his guest. The menu included cocktails made in a silver shaker with moonshine when he couldn't get gin. Truman was at Sam Rayburn's office sipping a drink with the House Speaker when he got the message of President Roosevelt's death, and he dashed out holding a tumbler as he rushed to the White House to be sworn in.

Eisenhower drank moderately. When he was president, Lyndon Johnson was known to come to the Capitol for an after-work swill with Senate Republican leader Everett Dirksen. I met Joe Califano, former secretary of Health, Education and Welfare, when I worked at a D.C. law firm in college, and he told me the story of visiting LBJ's ranch and riding around the property as the president drove, a station wagon of Secret Service agents following. Johnson drank scotch and soda out of a plastic cup, and when his cup was empty, he'd slow down and shake the cup out the window. A Secret Service agent ran up to the car and took the cup back to the station wagon where it was refilled with scotch, soda, and ice, and trotted back to deliver the fresh drink to LBJ's outstretched hand.

George W. Bush is infamous for his arrest in the 1970s for driving under the influence and for being drunk much of his time at Yale, even though he was reportedly a teetotaler while in the White House. Barack Obama liked a beer at a basketball game and a glass of white wine when he was out to dinner with wife Michelle.

It appears that the aroma of whiskey has flowered the air around Capitol Hill for two hundred years.

When my father left the Navy after WWII, he got a job working for the Navy Annex of the Pentagon just outside Washington. The suburbs around D.C. had blossomed and by the 1960s there were few forests left to hide illegal stills. My father resigned himself to paying the federal tax on a bottle of Old Granddad and staying out of trouble.

Drinking illegally has never been difficult. When I was seventeen, I obtained a fake driver's license. Georgetown bouncers didn't question that I might be a couple of years younger than the license stated. My first foray into a bar still haunts me. I was cute enough that men bought me drinks and naïve enough not to know when to say no. When I got home and my mother found me retching into the toilet, she put me to bed with a cool washcloth on my forehead—her treatment for the flu.

During Prohibition, there was no legal drinking age. In fact, it was not illegal to consume intoxicating beverages, but one could be arrested for manufacturing, transporting, or selling them. I would not have needed that fake ID to get into a speakeasy, but I might have needed a password or a name that opened a door to the bar.

Three hundred licensed bars sold liquor in the District of Columbia before Prohibition. In 1917, after Prohibition laws were put into effect in the District—three years before they were enacted nationwide—the number of underground liquor establishments numbered three thousand. Hooch was served at the best addresses, reports author Kim Roberts in her book *Prohibition Years*. For those who wanted to imbibe, Prohibition meant that alcohol was now unregulated, partiers could drink on the sly, and whiskey makers could rake in a killing.

Congress had its own bootleggers, and George Cassiday was the most popular among them. Known as "The Man in the Green Hat," Cassiday bought the liquor from a distiller in New York and took the train to Washington, lugging bottles of moonshine in a suitcase. Between 1920 and 1930, he did so much business on Capitol Hill that he had his own office in the building. Cassiday estimated that four out of five senators and representatives drank liquor, and he joked that the number of "dry" senators could fit into a taxicab. During that time the route between the Capitol building and the White House was known as Rum Row, according to Office of the Clerk, U.S. House of Representatives Historical Highlights.

Although Cassiday was arrested and convicted for his part in an illegal liquor business, he never spent a night in jail, thanks to his friends in high places.

When I was a student at George Washington University, I studied in the awe-inspiring Main Reading Room of the Library of Congress. In the stately Great Hall, Corinthian columns hold up arches supporting a gilded ceiling with intricate stained glass windows that let light shine onto the marble floor inlaid with brass. Frescoes float on the walls, including one of the goddess Artemis, the personification of temperance, pouring wine into a drinking bowl. For the classics, temperance meant moderation, not abstinence.

During Prohibition, alcohol was deemed so evil that it was banned from the general public except when prescribed by a doctor or used by priests and rabbis for sacred purposes. However, foreign embassies could host cocktail parties, and trucks hauling cases of liquor backed up to their doors and unloaded with impunity. There was a great deal of unloading at basement establishments and private residences as well. At the Gaslight Club on K Street, drinking members found the third-floor bar by entering through a faux men's bathroom. By turning a faucet handle, a sliding panel opened, admitting the privileged to the barroom. Archibald's Gentleman's Club, also on K Street, is now a strip club, but ninety years ago it was a residence turned speakeasy. Another establishment, The Little Green House, was operated by the Ohio Gang, a group of politicians and industry powerful who rubbed elbows with President Warren Harding. Harding looked askance as the cronies engaged in scandals and corruption under the leadership of lobbyist Howard Mannington, a jowly man in his late forties who dressed in tailored suits with a tiepin of diamonds and sapphires. Mannington was a smooth talker who carried a walnut walking stick and oversaw Little Green House as speakeasy, gambling house, and brothel. Liquor was delivered twenty cases at a time in a Wells Fargo truck accompanied by a man carrying a revolver and a badge that identified him as a federal agent, writes author Angela Eng. The parties were renowned for being jovial and lively, and it is rumored that a woman was killed by glass slivers when a jealous rival threw a champagne coupe at her. In addition to drinking, Little Green House was known as a venue for purchasing pardons and procuring appointments to federal office.

One federal officer, Gaston Means, worked for the Bureau of Investigation, which later became the FBI. Means's salary was seven dollars a day, on which he supposedly supported his family, three servants, a chauffeur for his Cadillac, and a townhouse on 16th Street— a block from the Department of Justice. Means was a large man with a balding pate. Biographer Francis Russell describes him as "a wastrel cherub with round face, dimpled smile, sharp chin, and beaming eyes that flickered from time to time with madness . . . a swindler for the joy of swindling, a liar proud of the credibility of his lies, a confidence man able to make his cheats and deceptions works of art."

When at home, Means worked in his basement office, equipped with desk and chair, two telephones, a filing cabinet, and a fireplace that he used for burning papers he didn't want to fall into the wrong hands. The laundry room contained white enamel washtubs he kept filled with ice to chill champagne, liquor and wine bottles.

But it was Means's back yard that was of particular interest. One entered into a steel cage through a locked gate thick as a bank vault. Another locked door led from the cage through a fence lined with double iron netting thirty feet high and camouflaged with vines. A square hole several feet wide held a hollow pipe that extended twenty feet into the ground, and inside the pipe was a steel box attached to a rope. In this subterranean safe deposit vault, Means kept money supplied by his illegal business dealings. At one point he hid as much as five hundred thousand dollars in the vault and estimated that seven million dollars passed through his hands.

Means was recognized as a bootlegger, blackmailer, forger, swindler and con artist. In 1917 he was arrested for the murder of a wealthy matron from whom he stole hundreds of thousands of dollars when he was acting as her business manager. The defense put together a local jury who sided with Means, and he was acquitted of the charge. Fifteen years later he conned a large sum from an heiress who asked him to help find the kidnapped Lindbergh baby. When Means absconded with the money, the heiress had him arrested, and he died in Leavenworth prison while serving a fifteen-year sentence.

■   ■   ■   ■   ■

Growing up, I was oblivious to whiskey's history. I knew people drank. We had a neighbor who worked for the Anheuser-Busch Brewery in the southwest section of Washington and brought home cases of beer he guzzled while sitting by his picture window, watching kids play outside. A few Saturday afternoons I went with my father to the Pimmit Grill and sat next to him on a bar stool drinking a Coke while he sipped glasses of beer. But Sunday was family day at home.

On Sunday afternoons, there was nothing in this world like the smell of my mother's pot roast wafting through the house. She'd put the roast on before church, and when we came home, it was ready for the potatoes, onions and carrots to be added to the juice in the pot. I'd watch her roll out dough for fresh biscuits, my mouth watering as the aroma of the baking delights mingled with the smells of meat and vegetables. I could hardly wait for dinner at 1:00 p.m., and later that evening my brothers and I had a supper of cold biscuits (she always made more than we could eat at dinner) fork split and stuffed with pieces of leftover meat. In honor of those Northern Virginia Sundays, here is a recipe for a pot roast like my mom used to make, this one with moonshine redolence.

Bootlegger Pot Roast in Whiskey Coffee Gravy

Prep time: 20 minutes
Cook time: 3 hours, 30 minutes

Ingredients:
1/2 cup flour
1/2 teaspoon salt
1/2 teaspoon freshly ground black pepper
4 to 5-1/2 pound beef chuck roast, trimmed of excess fat
1/4 cup vegetable oil
4 bay leaves
1 teaspoon dried thyme
2 cups water
2 cups freshly brewed coffee
1 large onion, quartered
2 carrots cut into 2-inch pieces
2 potatoes quartered
For gravy:
1 tablespoon flour
2 tablespoons butter, chilled
1/4 cup whiskey (or more, to taste)
Salt and freshly ground pepper to taste

Preparation:
Preheat oven to 325 F.
On a large plate, stir together flour, salt and pepper. Dust the beef with the seasoned flour. Heat the oil in a large, ovenproof pot over medium heat. Add the roast and brown on all sides, 5 minutes a side. Add bay leaves, thyme, water and coffee. Bring to a simmer, stirring and turning to combine the seasonings with the roast. Cover and place the pot in the oven. Bake for 2-1/2 to 3 hours or until fork tender. Add onion, potatoes and carrots and bake for another 30-45 minutes or until vegetables are

tender. Remove the meat and vegetables to a platter and cover loosely with foil to rest while you make the gravy.

To prepare the gravy, place the pot over medium heat, skim off excess fat and add water, if necessary, to deglaze the pot and equal 2-1/2 cups liquid. Whisk in the flour and cook 5 minutes, stirring until smooth and thickened. Stir in the butter and whiskey and season with salt and pepper.

Slice the meat, surround with the vegetables. Serve the gravy in a gravy boat or pitcher to pour over the roast slices.

Serve with mashed potatoes and fresh homemade biscuits.

Yield: 6 to 8 servings.

Chapter 6 ~ Make Shine While the Moon Glows

Love makes the world go round? Not at all. Whiskey makes it go round twice as fast.
~ Compton Mackenzie, British author

My family's weekend cabin is nestled in Virginia's Jefferson National Forest just yards from the Appalachian Trail. It's a perfect location for an illegal operation. Moonshining is concentrated in the mountains where the roads are steep and bumpy, where an old vehicle labored under a heavy load of corn, and where, without doubt, my Shenandoah Valley ancestors dabbled in the art of intoxication. Why wouldn't my nandaddy or great uncle divert feed corn—backbreaking work to plant and harvest— and employ alchemic know-how to produce a lucrative amber elixir?

Here's how they would have done it.

Pick a trail overgrown with briars and poison ivy, making it all but impassable. Tread slowly, carefully, to break as few stems as possible. Weave sharp laurel branches into the briars so there can be no quick charge. Fell a hemlock across the way—its leaves will be a green screen for the next year, even in winter.

Choose a cloudy night. Fog is even better—the mist will obscure the fire's smolder. For the fire use cypress, a softwood that doesn't give off much smoke. If there are stars, the Big Dipper will point north, where the moonshine will go to seek its fortune. But don't allow the moon. Or if the moon must shine, a gibbous moon is best, hanging as a sliver of light.

By a clear spring, set up your equipment—pots, copper piping, spigots, etc. You'll want clean clear water that runs cold from the mountains. Keep silent. The only sounds should be the gurgle of water over rock, a rustling of leaves in the breeze, the creak of crickets. There will be the sticky smell of pawpaw and honeysuckle, the taste of copper on the air, the sour sweet flavor of mash fermented for eight patient days.

Think it'd be easier to set up your still in the comfort of an old barn, a tarpaper shack, or a cramped kitchen? Think again. Any alcohol that is 80 proof or higher is flammable, so you'll need plenty of ventilation. Once in a while, mountain men trying to keep their business out of sight of revenuers inside a shed or an underground bunker have been known to blow up themselves and their operation, injuring the distiller, ruining his investment, and saving federal agents time and legwork.

A chief motivation for making moonshine—besides social drinking—is to escape taxes and regulations on alcohol manufacture and purchase. The ATF inspectors aren't around to make sure the moonshiners wash their hands after using the restroom (what restroom?), and moonshiners are not known for their sanitary habits. Who's to ensure that the ingredients are free of toxins and that no insects or even small animals tumble into the mash while it's fermenting?

Of course, the mash is not for drinking and, anyway, a fly or a wasp is not going to kill you. There isn't anything inherently dangerous in drinking moonshine if it's made properly—at least, no more dangerous than any other alcoholic drink. Although the general process for making moonshine is much the same as the way it's done in commercial distilleries, there are a few reasons why drinking illegal liquor can be a gamble.

Moonshine carries a hard taste because it hasn't been aged. Very potent, at 180 proof, or 80% alcohol, moonshine is strong enough to double as an effective cleaning agent. At 200 proof, you're drinking 100% alcohol. According to author Max Watman, the famous moonshiner Popcorn Sutton once said of moonshine between 180 and 200 proof, "It'll burn the hair off a wooden leg."

Since making moonshine is in my blood, I figured I ought to try my hand at distilling a batch. In most states, it's legal to brew a small amount of beer, but federal law prohibits distilling the mash into even a drop of liquor.

There's a brewing supply shop near my home, and I went there to buy materials. The smell inside was warm and earthy, caramel sweet, like a deep, mossy forest. Floor to ceiling shelves were packed with accoutrements for making brews of one kind or another. This was the exordium, the cradle of inebriation. Here were stocked the spermatozoa waiting to fertilize the egg that would hatch a raucous party—various flavors of hops, malt, barley, yeast, and syrups for sweetening. I felt intoxicated as soon as I walked through the door. My mind went blank. Why hadn't I brought a list of what I needed—like the mash fermenter, the boiler, the worm pipe, the slobber bucket, the hydrometer?

In the back, a bookcase held a few volumes instructing brewers in the skill of beermaking, but I saw nothing about how to distill whiskey. The only employee was a friendly looking fellow behind the counter, and I waited while the customer ahead of me paid for brewing materials.

"Credit or debit?" the clerk asked.

"Whatever's easier for you," the man said.

"Want a bag?"

"Don't need one."

Transaction finished. Beer brewers are basic folks.

My turn.

"I want to make some moonshine," I told the clerk.

He took a step back and crossed his arms.

"That's not our business," he said.

"I just want to build a still," I said.

He scowled. "We don't sell equipment for stills."

He pointed to the shelf of books.

"There's a book showing how to make a still."

It was the only volume in the bookcase relating to whiskey.

"I can buy a still on eBay," I said.

"Then that's what you should do."

I explained that I was doing research for a book and needed to distill just a little whiskey to be sure I understood the procedure.

"We sell beer-making equipment here," he said. "What you do with it is your business."

I could tell he was warming up to me.

"I'm pretty clear on how to get to the mash stage," I told him. "But I want to go the distance, if you know what I mean."

He looked around, checked the door.

"For all I know," he said, "you could be from the ATF." I knew he meant the agency that enforces liquor laws, among other things.

"I'm not from the ATF," I said. "I'm just trying to make a tiny bit of moonshine like my ancestors did."

"Right." His arms were still crossed defensively. He was looking down his nose, protecting himself—and his business. "I'm afraid I can't help you."

I should have been more prudent, more discreet, and not have mentioned "still" and "liquor."

I thanked the clerk and left.

Even though I won't be distilling hooch, I have a pretty good idea of how it's done. Copper is the best material because it conducts heat well and doesn't leach into the alcohol. But copper oxidizes and has to be cleaned each time it's used. And there are other dangers, like ergotism, methane poisoning, and several other kinds of poisons generated in the distillation process that can cause blindness or psychosis or can kill you. Which convinces me that my moonshine-making kin had to be pretty smart to get a still up and running and siphon off a product that was drinkable without being toxic.

There are two procedures in making moonshine—fermentation and distillation. Fermentation is the chemical reaction that occurs when yeast breaks down sugar. The sugar comes from corn, but white sugar can be added to ramp up the alcohol levels.

Great-uncle Bures Paxton used a submarine still, a horizontal metal cylinder as big as a sofa, large enough for a profitable run of liquor. He and his buddies built a wood fire under the cylinder to heat his mash.

Modern distillers favor propane, which is easier to regulate with less smoke to give away the location. There are lots of recipes, most of which include corn, either frozen or freshly cut from the cob. Nine pounds ought to be enough for a batch sufficient to share with friends. Add three pounds of cornmeal and seven gallons of water to a kettle—copper or stainless steel works well. Use distilled water rather than tap water to insure purity. Stir well while warming the mixture to just short of boiling and then turn off the heat and add a can of malt extract, the yeast used in beer making. Keep stirring. If you want a minty flavor to your hooch, toss in a little birch bark at this stage.

A moonshiner has to be patient enough to let his witches' brew soak up to several days while the starch in the corn converts to sugar. Check the density of the mash with a hydrometer. It should float when the brew is ready.

When making beer, carbon dioxide gas provides the fizz, but in distilling liquor, the gas is cooked away. For distillation, you'll need a workhorse of a boiler. It has to be rugged because, heated by an open flame and taxed by the corrosiveness of the mash, the boiler takes a lot of abuse.

For small batches, a boiler can be made by converting used restaurant pots, stainless steel wash pails, bakers dough pans, used beer kegs or such things, but modification requires welding to make proper connections. You'll also need a way to take the apparatus apart for cleaning. In order to distill the liquid, the boiler needs to be closed airtight with a pipe, called a cap arm, leading from the lid (also welded airtight) into the worm.

This is where things get technical and makes me think my grandpas and great uncle might have missed their calling as chemists. The distillation process involves evaporating the alcohol, which boils at 173 degrees, a lower temperature than water, and collecting the steam before condensing it back into liquid form. This same method is used for making expensive French perfumes and other aromatic spirits. Alcohol becomes vapor at forty degrees cooler than water. At 173 degrees, alcohol rises, leaving the water behind. Keep a close eye on the temperature. If the still is too hot, water or toxins can boil off and condense, leaving you with a watered-down liquor not fit to drink.

Most moonshiners use a heated barrel into which the steam is forced. The barrel is known as a thump keg because bits of the solid material from the mash can be carried on the steam, and the chunks of mash make a thumping sound when they drop to the bottom. The thump keg re-evaporates the alcohol, filtering out the mash on its way to the worm pipe.

The worm is a pipe that leads from the boiler and coils in a spiral, curving wormlike down through the worm box, a cask of cold water often diverted from a nearby stream. The fresh mountain water flows into the top of the barrel and out the bottom to keep the water constantly circulating, condensing the steam back into liquid form. Revenuers in the backwoods were known to walk down a creek or stream from one illegal still to the next, another reason to be sure the business is covert from all angles.

Potent liquid will drip from a spout or tap attached to the end of the coiled pipe. Before you catch the alcohol in a jar or bucket, set up a filtering system. A charcoal filter gives a purer product, but coffee filters can be used. Even if you filter the batch, it's very important to pour out the first few ounces of liquid—called the "foreshot"—that drip from the worm pipe. Methanol vaporizes before ethanol and is the first compound to condense in the still, so the foreshot contains most of the methanol from the mash. Methanol can cause blindness, paralysis, and death, and that first shot glass of hooch is a wise waste. One pass through the still may not be enough to create a safe batch. It takes two or three passes to remove the impurities from the alcohol.

My favorite local watering hole operates a microbrewery, and the brewmaster is a talkative fellow who knows more about the beer brewing business than I can absorb in one sitting. In his younger days, the brewmaster made whiskey, too, and he tells me that distillers refer to the "heads, hearts and tails" of a batch. When those first couple of ounces drip out, a moonshiner puts his eye to the rim of the glass. If his eye tears up, there's methanol in the whiskey and it must be discarded.

When the whiskey no longer brings tears to the eye, you have the "hearts" of the whiskey—that's the good stuff. When the condensation is nearly at its end, the whiskey will start to taste bitter—that's the "tails," and it's time to close up shop until the next run.

It's prudent to test the whiskey before you drink it. Pour a bit into a spoon and set it alight. A methanol flame is invisible, making the toxin nearly impossible to detect—another reason to discard those first precious ounces. A safe distillate burns with a blue flame, but if the liquor is tainted, the flame burns yellow. A trace of lead will give off a reddish flame. As they say in still culture, "Lead burns red and makes you dead." If the liquor doesn't flame at all, you may have distilled at too high a temperature. Another test is to pour moonshine into a jar and shake it. A bad batch will bubble up and hold the foam, but good shine will settle quickly.

Now that you've collected the condensed liquid and found it palatable, you're ready to present it to your guests. Forget oak casks for aging the spirits. Moonshine is sold—and drunk—as fast as it's made. Aged whiskey is expensive not only because of the federal taxes on the stuff but because so much of it evaporates while it's mellowing—often for a decade or more.

White lightning is a clear fluid but before bottling, fruit can be added for color and flavor. The "bottles" traditionally are canning jars in pint, quart or gallon sizes—whatever your market demands.

Making whiskey is not as simple as it may seem. Moonshiners go to a lot of trouble for a few gallons of the potent elixir. Is it worth it? History tells us it is. For centuries, offering a guest a drink has been common courtesy. Whiskey has helped celebrate marriages and births, welcome newcomers, and toast the harvest. Even today a host would be remiss not to have a supply on hand—legal or otherwise—to offer guests.

■   ■   ■   ■   ■

Harper Lee's novel *To Kill a Mockingbird* is narrated by the wide-eyed and tomboyish Scout Finch, a six-year-old girl. The story is set in Alabama during the Depression and, as history tells it, there had to be moonshine available. The only real drinker in the novel is the racist and violent Bob Ewell, not a man any respectable imbiber wants to emulate. But southerners like their whiskey. When a celebration is in order, the solution to getting a little tight without losing class status is to bake a Lane cake. The whiskey-soaked, multi-layered confection is a Deep South tradition dating back to the 1800s and is brought out for most any kind of festivity.

In Lee's novel, Maudie Atkinson is renowned for her free spirit and her delicious Lane cakes loaded with moonshine. After having a slice, Scout comments that it was "so loaded with shinny it made me tight." "Shinny," a code word for moonshine, is used liberally in the recipe.

Lane Cake is said to have originated in Clayton, Alabama, when its creator, Emma Rylander Lane, won a prize with it in the state fair. I've made this cake for company several times and advise a light dinner before serving the high-calorie dessert. If the alcohol doesn't produce an ever-so-slight sense of elation, the sugar will.

Lane Cake

(via Diana Baker Woodall)
Hands-on time: 1 hour 30 minutes
Total time: 15 hours 35 minutes

Ingredients for the cake:
1 cup (2 sticks) butter, softened at room temperature
2 cups granulated sugar
1 teaspoon vanilla extract
3-1/4 cups cake flour
3-1/2 teaspoons baking powder
¼ teaspoon salt
1 cup milk
8 egg whites
Ingredients for the filling and topping:
8 egg yolks
1-1/4 cups granulated sugar
Grated rind of 1 orange
1/3 cup whiskey (or more, if you like)
½ teaspoon mace
1-1/4 cups pecans, chopped
¼ teaspoon salt
1 cup shredded coconut
1 cup raisins
1 cup maraschino cherries, quartered

Preparation"
Preheat oven to 375 degrees. Grease and flour three 9-inch round cake pans.
Cream butter and sugar together until light and frothy. Beat in vanilla. Sift together flour, baking powder and salt. Sift again. Stir flour mixture into batter alternately with milk. Beat egg whites until stiff but not dry. Stir one-quarter of the whites into batter. Fold in remaining whites until just mixed.

Spoon batter into the 3 prepared cake pans and bake 20 to 25 minutes. Cool in pans for 10 minutes; turn onto cake racks.

To prepare filling, mix together yolks, sugar, and orange rind in a heavy pan or in the top of a double boiler. Cook over medium heat, stirring constantly until sugar dissolves and mixture thickens enough to coat the back of a spoon. Do not allow to boil or eggs will scramble. Remove from heat and stir in remaining ingredients, including the whiskey. Let filling cool. Spread between cake layers and on top and sides of cake.

Note: Lane cake improves in flavor as it ages and mellows. Covered and uncut, this cake can be made one week before serving. It's not necessary to refrigerate.

Yield: 10-16 servings.

Chapter 7 ~ Moonshine Blues

"Jake leg, jake leg, what in the world you trying to do?
Seems like everybody in the city's messed up on account of drinking you."
~ "Jake Liquor Blues," Ishmon Bracey, 1930

The geography around my family's cabin in Arcadia, Virginia, would have made it hard for federal agents to find a still unless they were willing to deal with rattlesnakes, copperheads, and thickets wiggling with ticks. When the Jefferson National Forest was part of the vast Appalachian wilderness, Indians competed with puma and wolf in the hunt for elk, buffalo and deer. We always see deer when we're weekending at the cabin, and if we're lucky enough, we catch a glimpse of a black bear. Walking along the Appalachian Trail, I keep an eye open for wild things.

One morning the trail was shadowed under a canopy of summer leaves. I worried about bulky mammals taking me by surprise as they scavenged for berries and grubs. Suddenly I stepped into a circle of light. Curved awkwardly, a sloppy S in the sun's spotlight, was a snake, rattle at one narrow end.

First, freeze.

Second, step back. Slowly.

Third, keep eyes open.

A golden-brown color, diamond pattern on its dry skin.

Don't snakes coil themselves before they strike? No coiling with this one. No rattling warning.

Looking closer, I saw that someone had taken care of matters, chopped off the snake's head and left the stringy corpse as warning:

there are dangers in this forest—a sting, a puncture, a poisonous surprise.

If you're not vigilant, lots of things can kill you. A city bus, a virulent virus, a drunk driver, a falling meteor, or homemade liquor. With moonshine, the aim is to get buzzed without getting poisoned.

Nobody drinks moonshine liquor for the taste. The rebellious drink it out of defiance. But mostly what you want is the punch. That punch, though, sometimes comes not from the high alcohol content but from the stuff moonshiners add to improve the taste, add color, and ramp up the proof if the distillation hasn't produced a quality liquor. Manure and fertilizer speed up fermentation. Formaldehyde masks the merciless flavor. Embalming fluid, bleach, rubbing alcohol and even paint thinner raise the alcohol level.

Common lye disguises the proof of the spirits. A high quality of lye is used to cure foods like green olives and to preserve others, like those inexpensive ramen noodles we ate in college days when we couldn't afford anything else. A little boiling water and we had a filling meal, if a bit corrosive to our digestive tracts. But it's doubtful that fellows making liquor in the woods over the past years had access to food-grade lye. Lower grades of lye are used to clean ovens and unclog drains, and that's most likely what found its way into the shine. Any of these wicked additives will do you in. If you're considering purchasing a jar of moonshine, I suggest you ask about the ingredients and check out the integrity of the source.

Back in the days when car radiators were used to heat the mash into a vapor, enough lead might end up in the moonshine to blind or kill the consumer. At one time, the still's pipes were welded with lead, and lead affects the central nervous system, causing mood swings, memory loss, and pain in the arms and legs. Reports of old-timers becoming psychotic from lead poisoning have been traced back to a contaminated still. If a drinker passed out either from high lead levels or too much liquor, his friends gathered around to tend him until it was determined whether he had died or was just "dead drunk." The vigil, known as a "wake," was held in case the deceased came to; otherwise, he was carted off to the graveyard.

Lead poisoning has been around since the Middle Ages but became epidemic in the twentieth century with the Industrial Age, according to author Sven Hernberg. When the automobile became fashionable in the 1920s, lead was added to gasoline to reduce engine knocking. Lead contained in auto emissions and in house paint became the main contributors to the public health problem of lead poisoning. Since these sources of lead were ubiquitous, hooch drinkers might have mistaken the alcohol itself as the culprit for their symptoms.

If lead weren't bad enough, car radiators that hadn't been cleaned properly might contain antifreeze residue. Antifreeze tastes sweet, which is why children and dogs are tempted to drink it. But beware. The first symptoms of poisoning are dizziness, slurred speech, confusion and vomiting—similar to drunkenness, which makes antifreeze poisoning hard to detect. If left untreated, there is liver failure and, ultimately, death. One ounce of antifreeze will kill a sixty-pound dog when the ethylene glycol crystallizes in the liver. Ironically, the treatment for a dog or cat that has licked up a puddle of spilled antifreeze is to get it to the vet's office within the first two hours after imbibing the stuff and to inject it with a large dose of ethanol. In other words, get a canine or feline sloshed and the alcohol will break down the crystals before they have a chance to choke the liver.

Earlier I mentioned discarding the foreshot, which contains most of the methanol generated when sugars are fermented from grain starches. Unprincipled distillers, however, will add cheap methanol to their shine to give it more kick. If you ingest methanol, your fingertips and lips will turn blue and you'll have trouble breathing. Your vision will blur, you'll have abdominal cramps and diarrhea, you'll be agitated, and you might go into convulsions.

And yet, those desperate for the high willingly suffer these effects by drinking denatured alcohol, which is traditionally 10% methanol, enough to get you pretty sick. Dan Baum writes in a *New Yorker* article that in the early twentieth century, rubbing alcohol was not subject to tax. To keep citizens from drinking it, in 1906 Congress passed laws mandating that ethyl alcohol not produced for beverages be poisoned to render it unfit for drinking. Unfortunately, that only succeeds in making denatured alcohol cheap—it doesn't prevent desperate partiers from spiking their punch with it or, worse, trying to purify it by distilling it themselves. Methanol evaporates at approximately the same temperature as ethanol and is impossible to separate.

Around Christmas 1926, hospital emergency rooms in New York City were deluged with people coming in with hallucinations and severe illness. Within a few days, two dozen had died. Whiskey wasn't available on store shelves, but denatured alcohol was. By 1933 when Prohibition ended, over ten thousand people had died because of government poisoning of rubbing alcohol, Baum says.

Legal liquor is manufactured from corn, barley, rye and other grains. George Washington preferred a liquor that was mostly rye, a drier drink than bourbon. But if not distilled properly, rye can cause ergotism, known in medical circles as a "cereal killer" because the fungus, ergotamine, has been found contaminating rye and wheat cereals. When ingested in large amounts, ergotamines constrict blood vessels, causing gangrene of the hands and feet. There will be hallucinations, psychosis, gastrointestinal distress, and a burning so painful that victims have felt as if they were being incinerated at the stake. If not treated, the toes and fingers can drop off, and even hands and feet turn black and separate from limbs. In medicinal use, doctors often prescribe tiny doses of ergot to help migraine sufferers. Ergot also constricts the uterus and can cause pregnant woman to miscarry. Not that a pregnant woman should be drinking rye whiskey. She might find ergotamines in rye bread, too. In fact, so many people innocently ate tainted rye bread in the Middle Ages that ergotism was epidemic and was called St. Anthony's Fire because of the burning sensation.

Stationed in the Pacific during the Second World War, my father enjoyed a cocktail when the ship docked in Shanghai. With other officers, he frequented the Cathay Bar housed in a well-appointed hotel now renamed Peace Hotel. One time, my dad was enjoying a few cocktails after having my mother's name tattooed inside a blue heart on his arm. He was in a merry mood, and the whiskey was cheap. The next morning, from his office as Chief Storekeeper aboard ship, he wrote to my mother, as he did weekly on his Underwood typewriter. The onionskin paper was so thin she could read a letter forward and then turn over the paper and read again backwards, as if looking for hidden messages. My father hit the keys so hard that the period poked a hole and when my mother held the paper to the light, it was like looking at stained glass. That clunker of a typewriter was a link to the world for my father, a door he could walk through to home, Virginia's Blue Ridge and the house perched on a mountainside along Covington's Magazine Street. I wish I had the typewriter now. I imagine words still inside it, waiting to be released.

"Well," he wrote one morning, "I have thought the matter over and believe I will live after all. When I came in here this morning, I had to clutch this typewriter with both hands to keep it from getting down on the deck and running around like a mad dog. That's why I'm not going to drink any more cocktails for a long time." That was a short-lived promise. Most sailors, including my father, drank liquor whenever they could find it.

Since 1914, alcohol has been banned from U.S. Navy ships except as medicine and then only when prescribed by a medical officer. And so the sailors have had to fend for themselves. Because of the dangers and constant anxiety, war takes its toll on military psyches. In submarines, with too many people crammed in too tight a space, claustrophobia can cause a sailor to dive over the edge of reason. For many, alcohol took their minds off the realities of their circumstances. Since there was no valium available in my father's day, drinking was a necessity to maintain sanity.

As officer in charge of provisions on his ship during World War II, my father had access to all the supplies on board. He kept the galley stocked with peanut butter and the bathrooms—the "heads"—with toilet paper, but I suspect the medicine cabinets were locked, the keys safely in the pockets of the medics. He had to be inventive if he wanted to sneak a drink.

When Dad was stationed at Pearl Harbor, there were plenty of lounges and grills where he and his buddies could get a cocktail. When he shipped out, he left a lot of his friends behind, telling them to hold tight and enjoy the palm trees, the turquoise waters and the hula girls. That was a week before the bombs fell. When he learned of the bombing of ships anchored at Pearl Harbor, Dad immediately wanted a drink to ease the grief of losing his comrades and to temper the relief he felt at his close call with disaster. Once he sailed west, however, his chances of getting a dram of alcohol were zero to impossible. There were no cocktail lounges aboard ship and if they dropped anchor near a remote island, it was doubtful they would find an exotic tropical bar. Superior officers monitored every action of the enlisted men. But military men are ingenious.

Sailors manning torpedoes on submarines and destroyers were in positions to sneak slugs of the pure grain alcohol that fueled the torpedoes. A sneak didn't amount to much, but if a sailor could manage to collect a bunch of sneaks into a stashed bottle or jar, he could host a surreptitious cocktail party.

The torpedoes were powered by miniature steam engines burning 180 or 190 proof ethanol as fuel. During the Pacific War, to keep enlisted men from drinking the fuel, the alcohol was denatured with 10% "pink lady," a blend of dye, methanol, and other ingredients. But the commanders hadn't figured on clever and resourceful sailors. "Torpedo Juice" was made by slicing the heels off a loaf of bread and compressing the loaf to manufacture a rudimentary fuel filter. Pour the fuel into one end and squeeze. What comes out the bottom may not be Tanqueray, but it's drinkable—with perhaps a few annoying side effects.

Torpedo juice cocktails were made by mixing the filtered alcohol with grapefruit, orange or pineapple juice. The liquor itself was colorless and tasteless but at 190 proof, the first swallow gave an electrifying jolt. One sailor said it felt like being kicked by a mule.

Marines at Guadalcanal looked to their compatriots from Tennessee to show them how to purify the fuel. The southern boys had grown up around stills and scrounged up copper tubing, a burner and a coffee maker to do the job. To separate out the pink lady from the fuel, at night in the foxholes they ran the liquid through their makeshift still. The "Torpedo Juice" website explains that the homemade liquor came in handy in at least one case when a military pharmacist was ordered to perform an emergency appendectomy aboard a submerged submarine. He sanitized his rubber gloves by dipping them in the torpedo moonshine, and the operation was a success.

When sailors got sick or went blind from methanol poisoning, military doctors reckoned that the U.S. government shouldn't be helping the enemy kill off its own men. They suggested another avenue to render the fuel unsavory. Croton oil, a laxative, was substituted for the methanol, and hot peppers were added as a further deterrent. Croton oil comes from the seeds of a tree that grows in India and Malaysia. When processed, the oil acts as a powerful purgative and irritant, causing severe diarrhea and skin lesions. When ingested, a single drop of croton oil almost immediately gives a person the shits. An overdose induces intestinal inflammation, pain, vomiting, bloody stools and ultimately death, according to the site Ship's Diary of USS Hayward L. Edwards.

Before the oil was discovered to be poisonous, it was prescribed by doctors for patients with bowel problems. Today croton oil is used by dermatologists in skin peel treatments. The oil made its way into literature when John Steinbeck, in his novel *East of Eden,* had his character Kate sneak croton oil into the prostitute Faye's drinks to do her in so she could inherit Faye's whorehouse. In *Look Homeward Angel*, Thomas Wolfe has a farmer's wife spike a liquor bottle with croton oil to keep teenagers Gus Moody and Steve Gant from pilfering it. The boys were sick for days afterward.

W. E. Battenfield, who survived the Pearl Harbor attack, wrote of his experiences on the submarine USS *Pogy* in an online blog titled "Submarine Sagas." He explains that one chief had problems with regularity and every Monday morning before he inspected the torpedoes, he mixed a little torpedo juice into his coffee. A Japanese prisoner on board watched him and asked, "Sake?" The chief nodded yes and fixed the prisoner a drink made with the concoction. The prisoner asked for more. After four or five drinks, he began to sing happily. Afraid an officer would discover the prisoner's drunkenness, the chief sent him to his bunk. Within half an hour, the prisoner sprang from his bunk screaming, "Bonzi! Bonzi!"—the Japanese word for "Charge!" Battenfield was standing watch in the forward torpedo room armed with a .45 pistol in case prisoners revolted. When he saw the prisoner running madly toward him, he reached for his gun but the man dashed past him and headed straight for the head, where he alternated sitting and heaving. Battenfield later discovered that the prisoner was not yelling "Charge!" but "Benjo!"—a Japanese slang word for "toilet." The next morning when the chief made his coffee, Battenfield offered a mug to the prisoner, but he declined.

A sailor in need of alcohol is not easily denied. When enlisted men discovered that alcohol evaporates at a lower temperature than croton oil, they again devised crude stills to boil off the ethanol and condense it without the additive. The stills were referred to as Gilly stills—built by a sailor named Gilly, no doubt—and the distilled liquor became known as "gilly." Everyone agreed that when mixed with fruit juice, the alcohol was palatable.

Stories abound about the efforts of military men to have themselves a drink. When my father-in-law was stationed in the Middle East, he and his fellow Marines added raisins to water in a glass jar and set the jar in the sun for a few days to ferment. The same technique is used in jails when prisoners save their raisin ration to manufacture "jailhouse hooch." My ex-Marine father-in-law admits that the alcohol didn't taste very good and gave him a headache, but desperate circumstances require desperate measures.

Under an "Act to Promote the Efficiency of the United States Navy," the Navy issued a general order restricting the sale, serving or transport of liquor within a five-mile radius of any U.S. naval installation. But even that order could be circumnavigated by having a bootlegger set up shop on a boat just outside the restricted zone. An officer could then requisition a boat to motor out and conduct business.

After Prohibition ended, officers' clubs were permitted to serve liquor, but the constraint against alcohol on ships continues to this day.

For civilians in depressed neighborhoods during Prohibition, there was a different form of poison. It was an era of desperation that left poor men turning to whatever alcohol they could lay hands on, including rubbing alcohol, hair oil, and doctored antifreeze. In the 1930s, according to Baum, a hundred thousand unfortunates suffered paralysis of the legs from drinking "jake," a Jamaican ginger extract sold as a medicinal tonic for ills from catarrh and flatulence to late menstruation. Composed of 85% alcohol, it packed the wallop of four jiggers of scotch. Jake was cheaper than whiskey and had a higher alcohol content and although technically not moonshine, the Jamaican liquor was a way to get drunk on the cheap and avoid paying the federal liquor tax. Jake became the new binge drink for bums and drunks who lived alone in the seediest parts of towns.

At first, jake was innocent enough and when mixed with Coca-Cola or coffee, the strong ginger flavor went down easy. Then two Boston brothers-in-law, Harry Gross and Max Reisman, decided to profit from the liquor. They rented two floors of a building in downtown Boston and went full-time into the business of manufacturing the Jamaican ginger extract and shipping it in barrels around the country as "liquid medicine in bulk." When customers complained about the quality of the jake, Reisman and Gross discovered that an industrial chemical improved the flavor. Lindol, a tri-ortho-cresyl phosphate, was a flame retardant used in plastics and rubber and also sold as an insecticide. Assured by the chemical company that the solution was safe, they adulterated 640,000 bottles of their product and set off an epidemic of paralysis.

The paralysis outbreak swept across the country from the Northeast to the Midwest and down to Mississippi. "Jake leg," as the condition came to be known, caused victims to walk with a high-stepping, foot-slapping gait that became known as the "jake-leg walk."

During the first bout of jake-leg paralysis, references to jake started to appear in folk songs, like the Allen Brothers' "Jake Walk Blues" recorded in 1930:

> *I can't eat, I can't talk*
> *Been drinkin' mean Jake, Lord, now can't walk,*
> *Ain't got nothing now to lose,*
> *'Cause I'm a Jake-walkin' papa with the Jake walk blues.*

Willie "Poor Boy" Lofton's "Jake Leg Blues" first mentions the "limber leg."

> *I said, jake leg, jake leg, jake leg, tell me what in the world you gonna do*
> *I say, you done drunk so much o' that, oh Lord,*
> *'til it done give him the limber leg.*

The "limber leg" is mentioned in almost every blues song of the Depression era. The term was coined by women frustrated by their men's sexual impotence, an unfortunate side effect of the paralysis.

Author Eisha Zaid writes that doctors were stymied as to the cause of the ailment until they listened to the Allen Brothers, Ishmon Bracey, Tommy Johnson, the Mississippi Sheiks, Willie Lofton, and Daddy Stovepipe singing their songs about jake leg. Then they started to put the pieces together. A year after Gross and Reisman went into production, the two were arrested for conspiracy to violate federal law. They pleaded guilty and paid a $1,000 fine each but avoided prison time by vowing to lay the finger on the New York bootleggers they claimed had manufactured the tainted jake. When they couldn't produce the alleged bootleggers, Gross was slapped in jail for two years. Reisman went free.

The Guinness Book of World Records lists Everclear as the most alcoholic drink available on the legal market. At 190 proof, it is 95% pure grain alcohol and should be consumed with caution. When I was in high school, I attended an outdoor party on the edge of a wood in Northern Virginia. I didn't realize until later that the grape juice punch had been spiked with Everclear. I was with a friend who was driving his father's brand-new Oldsmobile Vista Cruiser wagon. I don't remember how much of the cocktail I consumed—I suspect it didn't take much to send me reeling. And if the punch affected my friend as it did me, I don't know how he drove his dad's sleek automobile. On the way home I asked him to pull over so I could look at the stars. A gentleman, he came around the car to open my door, and when I got out, I steadied myself with my hand on the door frame. He must not have seen my hand in the darkness and slammed the door shut, catching my thumb. I screamed, and he had to open the door to release my hand. The thumb didn't appear to be broken, but the end was smashed flat. I felt a throbbing but no pain until the next day when I woke with a headache, a dry mouth, and a thumb swollen as big as a plum. Needless to say, I lost the thumbnail, and to this day it grows in flat. Since then, I've learned to sip my drinks slowly and measure their effect with vigilance.

■　　■　　■　　■　　■

Over the years, my taste for alcohol has become more sophisticated. I've spent time in Kentucky, where I enjoy the caramel flavor of their bourbon. At the Brown Hotel in Louisville, the first lesson I learned is never to let an ice cube near a shot of fine bourbon. I drink it neat and even sneak a little into my cooking. Couple bourbon with pecans and butter, and you have a treat fit for the gods. The following simple recipe has a variety of uses, and you'll want to try them all. If you're so inclined, substitute walnuts for the pecans and whiskey for the bourbon.

Bourbon Pecan Sauce

Prep time: 5 minutes
Cook time: 10 minutes

Ingredients:
1 cup sugar
1/3 cup water
1/3 cup chopped pecans, toasted
2 tablespoons milk
1-1/2 tablespoons butter
1 tablespoon bourbon or whiskey
2 teaspoons vanilla extract

Preparation:
Combine sugar and water in a small saucepan. Cook over medium-high heat 5 minutes or until sugar dissolves, stirring constantly. Stir in milk, butter, bourbon, vanilla extract, and pecans. Reduce heat and cook 3-4 minutes or until mixture is thick and bubbly.
Serve over chicken, pork chops, pancakes, cheesecake, bread pudding or ice cream.
Yield: 1-1/4 cups.

Chapter 8 ~ Modern Moonshine

Alcohol is the anesthesia by which we endure the operations of life.
~ George Bernard Shaw

In 1934, Virginia was the first of the southern states to throw out the Prohibition law. Instead, it enacted the Alcoholic Beverages Control Act that set up dispensaries to sell liquor, wine, and beer at a price lower or equal to moonshine being sold by bootleg distillers. A customer could buy a quart of liquor from the state for $1.25. The aim was not to make money but to drive out bootleg operations, writer Bruce Stewart says in his book *Moonshiners and Prohibitionists: The Battle over Alcohol in Southern Appalachia*. The problem was laying in enough stock to supply the demand. When dispensaries sold out, customers went back to the bootleggers.

The ABC Act prohibited the public consumption of whiskey, which meant there were no saloons pushing shots across the bar—at least not legally. Hotel restaurants were limited to the sale of wine and beer. The theory may have been sound, but the application was a failure. The *New York Times* headline on April 1, 1934, read, "VIRGINIA WET AGAIN, BUT ALL IS BOOTLEG."

In the late 1960s, while I was in college I worked at a law firm in Washington, D.C. Richard Nixon had just been elected president, and the war in Southeast Asia was escalating. Martin Luther King's assassination set off riots, and I had watched the news in horror after the shooting of Bobby Kennedy. Time felt short. With the future uncertain, each of us was painfully aware of our mortality.

While I was struggling to keep up with my college classes, my friend Wendy was interested in getting high. She wore black tights, gray miniskirts and black turtlenecks. I thought she was smart and sophisticated, and I was flattered that she accepted me as a pal. One weekend we arranged to throw a party at my apartment in Arlington and were listening to Jefferson Airplane and the Doors while we got ready. Wendy had bought a bottle of scotch and handed me a shot in a tumbler of ice. It tasted disgusting—like moldy rubbing alcohol.

"Keep drinking," she said. "You'll get used to it."

I was trying to stomach the awful liquid when Wendy took a plastic bag from her backpack and sprinkled what looked like dried oregano onto a thin paper. I watched her roll the cylinder and lick the paper to keep the joint together. She lit the tip, drew in smoke and passed the joint to me.

"Inhale and hold it in as long as you can," she said.

Wendy had graduated from college the year before, and I wanted to be as wise and free as she was. I didn't smoke, but I took the joint and puffed, trying to hold in the smoke as she instructed. My throat burned. I coughed.

"Take another hit," she said.

Within seconds my hands started to sweat and my hair felt sticky against my neck. When she got up to pour herself more scotch, I dragged a stool into the hall closet and sat among the coats, spellbound by the pilly little nubs on the wool sleeves until guests began arriving.

The next morning, even as I bent over the toilet to throw up, I felt elated. I had stepped across a forbidden boundary. Pot was illegal, and I was too young to drink. It was like stealing second base or winning at dodge ball—if you get away with it, you've beaten the odds. Besides, everyone was smoking and drinking, or so it seemed, and drinking and smoking tightened my friendship with Wendy.

Unlike moonshine and other American whiskeys which are distilled mostly from corn, scotch is made from malted barley. The taste is decidedly different and I have never developed an appreciation for it. For Wendy, as for many young people, the attraction to alcohol and marijuana was as much the illegal adventure as the experience itself. If she had lived in another place at another time, I'm sure she'd have made moonshine herself and enjoyed a fair portion of her own product.

As a little girl, I used to go outside and twirl, my arms flying out, my skirt fanning up over my skinny thighs. I loved the way the sky revolved and the leaves on the trees spiraled above me. Dizzy and drunk on summer, I reeled and staggered and fell to the grass laughing. After a few minutes, when the world stopped looping, I got up and twirled again.

In Turkey, an order of Sufi Muslims known as the Malawi, founded by Rumi in the thirteenth Century, have a practice of spinning in a sort of dance as a way of reaching religious ecstasy. Dervishes, as the devotees are named, whirl in long white skirts that billow around them like frothy waves while musicians play and chant. Tourists and other outsiders are allowed to watch the whirling dervishes as long as they show reverence and respect, according to Soka Gakkai International.

I've often wondered about our desire to become intoxicated with a drug or a drink or an activity that changes our consciousness. According to Buddhist teacher Nichiren Daishonin, a contemporary of Rumi, there is a fundamental darkness to life, and maybe it is our need to mask the darkness that leads us to twirling and to intoxication.

Humans aren't the only earthly creatures with a propensity for drunkenness. Rainforests are aflutter with wobbly butterflies and fruit bats. Even elephants and primate species stumble after feasting on fermented fruit. On Barbados beaches, vervet monkeys—miniature primates with black faces and silver fur—steal cocktails from the tables of distracted vacationers, writes Robert Dudley in an article titled "Ethanol, Fruit Ripening, and the Historical Origins of Human Alcoholism in Primate Frugivory." They prefer fruity rum drinks over beer or wine. A study of a rhesus macaque social group, a species of monkey that resembles humans anatomically and physiologically, found that primates in the lab like to end the day with a cocktail. They drink when they feel stressed, and monkey lushes react much the way people do. When they imbibe enough to raise their blood alcohol above .08%, the legal limit for most states, they sway, stumble, and often vomit. In Panama, howler monkeys climb out onto limbs of the astrocaryum palm whose bright orange fruit at the peak of its ripeness gives off the smell and taste of alcohol. Never mind that the fruit clusters hover thirty feet above the forest floor—the taste and the buzz are worth the precarious risk.

What is our mammal cousins' attraction to hooch? For forty million years, monkeys have dined on ripe fruit. In their tropical forest home, yeasts in the fruit flesh and on its skin convert the sugars to ethanol, which emits a sweet aroma signaling ripeness. For a hungry monkey, the smell of alcohol triggers a drive to get to the fruit quickly and eat it before a competitor finds it. A ripe hanging fruit can have an alcohol content of 1%, but an overripe fruit fallen to the ground can contain as high as 4% alcohol. In one gorging session, a monkey can consume enough alcohol to equal ten cocktails, Dudley says. Maybe we haven't evolved so far from our biological relatives as we think.

Where I live in northern New England, cool autumn days ripen apples that tumble and ferment under apple trees, and wild turkeys feast on their alcoholic juiciness. Turkeys prefer to strut through fields in flocks rather than take to the air. After a session at an apple tree saloon, a turkey flies like a large piece of cardboard flapping in the wind. One late autumn I saw a turkey, startled by a passing police cruiser, fly up in an aerial totter and take out the light on the cruiser's roof, a fatal miscalculation that may well be attributed to tipsiness.

A study by Sarah Williams reported in *Science* magazine found that mice, rats and monkeys tend to drown their sorrows in alcohol when isolated or bullied by others of their species. When female fruit flies rebuff the sexual advances of male fruit flies, the study found, the males are more likely to drink from a straw containing 15% alcohol than are their sexually sated comrades who rehydrate after their coupling with plain sugar water. Once impregnated, female fruit flies lay their eggs in fruits of intoxicatingly delicious ripeness, and the baby flies are sweet hooch addicts the minute they're born.

When humans first appeared a million years ago, they chose a diet of meat and tuber roots over fruit, but in China, pottery dating back nine thousand years shows the dried residue of beer, suggesting that our Neolithic relatives imbibed now and then. They believed that alcohol was heaven's gift of inspiration. Beer was more a staple than bread, says Abigail Tucker in *Smithsonian*, and the Babylonians drank beer and worshipped a wine goddess. Egyptians have been drinking wine since 4,000 B.C.E., and the Old Testament tells us that Noah planted a vineyard on Mt. Ararat in eastern Turkey. He must have loaded grape seeds on the ark before rainfall with the idea of planting at the first opportunity.

Researchers have found that having a drink with food causes us to linger over our supper, consuming more calories—which was fortunate in the old days but in this age of sedentary lifestyle poses a waistline problem. So if you're going to drink while you eat, take out a gym membership.

It's a good idea, on the other hand, to eat while you drink so that your dinner will absorb some of the alcohol. With the growing market for artisanal foods—high quality, nonindustrial fare produced on a small scale—there's a crusade to recapture old gustatory traditions. Of the eight thousand breweries in the U.S. today, 90% are independent craft brewers who produce fewer than six million barrels of beer a year. There's also a rise in bars that offer classic cocktails, like a bistro I frequent where Jen the bartender concocts me her special ginger martini.

And then there's corn liquor. A whiskey aficionado might turn up her nose at a licensed distillery selling bottles of green whiskey—so young that it hasn't had time to develop a tanned complexion. And yet masses of people are buying these young whiskeys, either by the bottle or by the shot. Shine On Georgia Moon comes in a quart Mason jar with a screw-on lid, and the handmade-looking label boasts that the corn liquor is "Less than 30 days old." The moonshine-like liquid checks in at 40% ethanol or 80 proof, and a finger or two will go for ten bucks across the bar. You won't be hounded by revenuers because Georgia Moon is legal, even though its label misleads one into thinking the corn was produced in Georgia. Actually, it comes from HeavenHill Distilleries in Kentucky, which also sells fine rum, tequila, and bourbon. White Dog, a legitimate whiskey made by Kentucky's Buffalo Trace Distillers, has a slightly syrupy flavor because of the presence of rye in the mash, and at 125 proof White Dog has the highest alcohol content of the legal green whiskeys. In spite of the rummy taste, the clear elixir carries a burn reminiscent of a quaff fresh from a mountain still, author Max Watman says in his book *Chasing the White Dog: An Amateur Outlaw's Adventures in Moonshine*.

These distillers are aware of the nostalgia wafting from local history buffs and they aim to capitalize on it. But don't expect to be charmed by the flavor. You won't enjoy the mellow taste that comes from aging in charred white oak barrels. The corn liquor most likely never got near a barrel. And don't let the innocent clarity of the liquid fool you. One imbiber compared the taste to a belch after drinking water from a cheap garden hose, says Watman.

Selling illegal moonshine makes good economic sense. A superior tasting whiskey is aged at least two years in barrels that take up space and have to be rotated in the warehouse to compensate for fluctuations in temperature. And not only is the whiskey not bringing in money during that time, but the alcohol is seeping into the wood and evaporating. When the finest finally goes to market, the price for a bottle of legal liquor can be staggering—and half of the money goes to the federal government in taxes. Many moonshiners have considered applying for a license to sell their goods legally, but the regulations and the costs of licensing have sent them back to the deep woods.

If consumers want a taste of the spirit of old Appalachia, an enterprising distiller will provide the goods—except that hooch from a licensed distiller is legal, and legal hooch rubs against what moonshiners believe to be a God-given right to run their own stills on their own property. And then there's the fact that buying moonshine in a liquor store is anything but exciting. The excitement comes from breaking the law. And so moonshine running continues.

I was changing my health care coverage a while back and when I spoke with a representative by phone, I recognized his southern accent.

"Where are you?" I asked.

"Roanoke, Virginia," he said.

"Ah," I said. "The land of moonshine."

"Absolutely," he said. "Everyone down here has a jar stashed in a cupboard." He explained that it is still polite in his part of the country to offer a guest a shot of moonshine. "Moonshine is a boutique business," he said and added that a federal agent can tell by its taste who made the illegal distillate. He favors liquor infused with damson plum but has sampled apple shine that tastes just like apple pie.

For the most part, it appears that agents for the ATF turn a blind eye to minor moonshine operations. Nevertheless, every year illicit stills are seized in Maryland, Virginia, and the Carolinas. In Virginia, alcohol smuggling costs the state an estimated $20 million a year in tax revenue, and the Old Dominion has a permanent Moonshine Task Force. In the past few years, a crackdown on illegal liquor, dubbed Operation Lightning Strike (OLS), sent a few offenders to prison for sixty years. OLS broke up one multimillion-dollar ring that had run a moonshine business for over thirty years and supplied unlawful distillers with tons of sugar, bottling supplies and ingredients to produce thousands of gallons of hooch, writes Oliver Libaw in an article titled "Illegal Moonshine Is Still Flowing." Less ambitious moonshiners are looking at five years behind bars and a $10,000 fine for the first offense, varying by state, even if they don't plan to sell it. That's a risk producers are willing to take.

The biggest still ever seized in Virginia's Botetourt County, where my father grew up, was discovered in a 1987 raid. The distillers had a dozen 900-gallon capacity pots that produced 750,000 gallons of moonshine a year. Alcohol Beverage Control agents found 15,000 gallons of mash that distilled into 1,500 gallons of whiskey a week, Libaw says. Moonshiners are willing to gamble with getting caught because the penalties are lighter than they are for dealing drugs. The Botetourt outlaws were sentenced to three years in prison, an insignificant price to pay for getting rich quick.

There surely are lots of backwoods and barn stills dripping a profit, but federal agents suspect that fewer people are making trivial amounts and more are involved in larger and more professionally run businesses that deal in marijuana, methamphetamines, and stolen property. But bootleg whiskey is still big business in Appalachia. Lawbreaking entrepreneurs operate a network of dozens of eight-hundred-gallon stills that can gush out thousands of gallons of illicit liquor a week. Franklin County moonshine has been identified in Florida, New York, and as far away as California. Enterprising moonshiners sell to distributors who package the liquid merchandise in six-packs of plastic gallon jugs to sell in poor sections of cities where customers are willing to buy their remedy at half the price of its legal counterparts, says Libaw.

My Nida relatives eschewed these types of large illegal enterprises a long time ago. But residents of the Shenandoah Valley still like to quench their thirst with homemade whiskey. Either they have developed a taste for moonshine or they don't like the idea of paying taxes for their homemade liquor. Low cost and long tradition keep the illegal trade alive. And as long as there is demand, there will be supply.

The most famous moonshiner in recent days was Marvin "Popcorn" Sutton, a North Carolinian who set up his corn whiskey operation in Tennessee and published a book, *Me and My Likker*, detailing his moonshine business. Sutton's operation was the subject of a film documentary featured on the History Channel and won an Emmy in 2009. Popcorn made no bones about the fact that he produced the best whiskey in Cocke County, as if daring federal agents to storm his rustic cabin in the woods where he kept his stills. When the law caught up with him, Popcorn was arrested. Already ailing from lung cancer, rather than serving time in prison Popcorn hooked a hose to the tailpipe of his truck and asphyxiated himself, Watman writes. Just months after his death, Tennessee passed a law allowing microdistilleries to operate without a license. The first bottles off the production line in 2011 were made from a recipe Popcorn left behind and were labeled "Popcorn Sutton's Tennessee White Whiskey." A folk tradition at last had become legitimized.

In Shelburne, Vermont, a man named Nick Cowles owns a large apple orchard that has been in his family for generations. During Prohibition, his grandfather operated an illegal still. Everyone in the area knew he was making whiskey, and he did a brisk business with local residents. One winter night when the thermometer flirted with zero—the temperature when fingers go numb and nostril hairs freeze—Mr. Cowles, hankering after warmth, fanned the flames under the boiler. A spark shot up and kissed the dry wood of the shelter, catching it alight. When the structure flared up, Cowles's wife called the fire department, and a truck came sirening into Shelburne with two federal agents in its wake. The firemen knew Mr. Cowles and had an intimate relationship with his liquor. The agents stood by while the firemen put out the fire. Then, as the agents stepped in, the firemen turned the hoses on them. In bitter cold, a drenched man can suffer from hypothermia within minutes. Rather than taking the time to arrest Nick's grandfather, the agents went home to change into dry clothes so as not to freeze to death. When they returned, the still was gone, dismantled, done away with and, since the agents were not able to collect evidence, no arrest was made. The next day, when Nick's granddad came to check the damage, he found a dead crow lying where the still had been. He picked it up, took the crow to have it bronzed, and presented copies of the metal bird to the firemen who had saved his neck.

Nick followed his grandfather's example when he was just eighteen years old and started making illegal brandy from the orchard's apples. A few years ago he caved in and applied for a liquor license. He thought of labeling his brandy "Finally Legal" but decided instead on "Dead Bird Apple Brandy." He aged his first batch for eight years and when he offered it for sale at a hundred dollars a bottle, the entire run sold out immediately. He hopes to have a limited batch of bottles ready for sale every year.

In the eighteenth century, Vermont was dotted with breweries and micro-distilleries, but these were shuttered in the fervor of the state's temperance movement. Vermont banned alcohol in 1852, long before Prohibition. Just north on the Canadian border, a speakeasy with the moniker Bucket of Blood straddled the dividing line between countries, and Vermonters could get soused at the Canadian end of the bar drinking what the Canadians called *goût de terroir*, or "taste of the local," a homemade liquor said to be made from nearby springs with sugar from adjacent maple trees in stills heated with wood from the land.

Moonshine is produced all over the globe. A while back, I met a young American-born man who is the son of an Iranian father and a

Boston mother. His father died when he was a child, but every year he visits family in Iran. According to the young man, moonshine reaches its seductive hand all the way to the Middle East. Iran is a Muslim country, and the religion forbids drinking alcohol. But many Muslims nevertheless distill their own liquor—they call it *arak*—at home or in back rooms of warehouses. *Arak* is fermented with raisins and has a smooth flavor, our friend told us. The liquor he tasted had been distilled three times and run through a carbon filter. In the second distillation, aniseed is added to give the liquor a subtle flavor of licorice and tarragon. When I sampled a legal shot at a Middle Eastern restaurant in Massachusetts, it tasted much like a very strong anisette or pastis.

A true Iranian experience is a supper of roasted beef liver and heart sliced and skewered on a kebab. When the meat is tender, the kebab is folded into a broad piece of flatbread held tightly while the skewer is extracted.

"Delicious," our friend said, "especially chased with a drink made with *arak*."

Considering that the penalty for being caught with illegal liquor is severe—even death—a surprisingly large number of Muslims create their own moonshine. "The way it was during American prohibition," our Iranian friend told us, "is the way it is in Iran today." Public drunkenness is rare, and Muslims who partake in drinking moonshine do so in their homes. In spite of the danger, indulging is done with ceremony and delight. Danger, I suspect, is part of the enjoyment.

Around the globe, homemade liquor reflects the customs, tastes, and raw materials for fermentation available in each region. A friend who spent time in Romania had enjoyed Țuică, Romanian 120-proof moonshine made from plums and yeast, without sugar. Farmers have been known to hang a bottle on a plum tree so that the fruit grows into the container, saving a step in the process, he said. Țuică is distilled today as it always has been, in a brass still using wood heat. Although illegal, the government turns a blind eye because of the traditional nature of the drink. Romanians drink a shot before each meal and imbibe as a ritual at weddings and religious holidays. If you want to acquire a sample without paying the exorbitant tax for a bottle of the legal variety, you might be able to purchase an *ulcior*—a jugful—from a Romanian roadside vender in autumn, after the fruit harvest.

Moonshine vintages can have amusing names. In Nigeria, *ogogoro* is also known as "crazy man in a bottle." In Kenya, *changaa* translates to "kill me quick" because of the battery acid distillers use to add a strong boost to the drink. Saudi Arabians drink *siddiq*, meaning "friend." In Guatemala, when performing healing ceremonies shamans drink *cusha*, a slang term for brandy, and spit it on their patients. It's also customary for a young man to bring a carafe of *cusha* to his girlfriend's father when he comes to ask for her hand in marriage. The more *cusha* they drink, the more approving the dad is of his future son-in-law, author David Hanson writes in his article "History of Alcohol and Drinking around the World."

The point is, moonshine is not exclusive to Appalachia. Humans globally share a desire to socialize and be happy. And whiskey is often part of the merriment.

■   ■   ■   ■   ■

For Americans, the Christmas season is cause for parties and high spirits, wassail and spiked eggnog. Globes of bourbon-laced chocolate are a joy any time of the year, but they lend a festive air to the winter holiday season. Kentuckians wouldn't dream of celebrating Christmas without their delicious chocolate bourbon balls. The following recipe is a twist on Kentucky's famed treat but is made with whiskey. Substitute bourbon or a flavored liqueur if you prefer. One warning: Double the recipe because your friends will want to take home a batch of these delicious gems.

Chocolate Whiskey Balls

Prep Time: 30 minutes

Ingredients:
1 cup pecans
1 cup chocolate wafer cookie crumbs
1 cup confectioners sugar
1-1/2 tablespoons light corn syrup
1/4 cup whiskey
Powdered sugar for rolling

Preparation:
In a food processor, grind the pecans and chocolate wafers coarsely and scrape into a large bowl. Mix in the sugar, corn syrup, and whiskey. Use hands to shape into quarter-size balls and roll in powdered sugar.
Store in an airtight container in a cool place, or freeze on a baking sheet until each is firm and store in tightly sealed plastic bags.
Yield: 2 dozen

Afterword

My von Nida ancestors attended church services on Sunday and minded their own business. Peripheral information suggests that they, like their neighbors, produced their own liquor. They were not out to make a staggering profit from an illegal industry but wanted only to live quietly and benefit from a few of the pleasures life offers.

In researching this book, I discovered that alcohol touches us all. My husband's forebears were *Mayflower* passengers who enjoyed beer both on the voyage over and for nourishment once they settled at Plimouth Plantation. During Prohibition my husband's grandfather made vodka in his bathtub on Boston's North Shore. His parents still indulge in a cocktail before dinner. So do I. There's nothing wrong with that.

But there's a dark side to drinking alcohol. In the United States, fourteen million people are alcoholics, and abuse of alcohol is the third leading cause of preventable death. Today illegal liquor production can be a streamlined and practical business with warehouse distilleries and innocuous looking vans for distribution. The moonshine business can also be a gateway to felonious activity.

This book is not meant to encourage drinking or unlawful behavior but to offer a glimpse into the role illegal moonshine has played in this country. Appalachian moonshine legends have found their way into literature, music and film. Homemade liquor has influenced our history, politics, economics, culture, art and religions. Families made moonshine to support themselves during tough economic times, embodying independence and the rebel spirit. Stills were crude and simple or carefully crafted from oxidized copper with a patina of time. Some produced harmful intoxicants and others produced fine liquor.

Shakespeare speaks of liquor. The Bible speaks of wine. Many of the great writers of the last centuries have taken up the pen to write about alcohol. Whiskey is, inevitably and for better or worse, part of our lives. As English writer, scholar and historian George Saintsbury has said, "It is the unbroken testimony of all history that alcoholic liquors have been used by the strongest, wisest, handsomest, and in every way best races of all times." I'll drink to that.

Acknowledgments

Many people have lent a hand in getting this book onto the page. Jack Nida, a member of our clan, has written a sixteen-hundred-page book documenting Nida ancestry. Mr. Nida has identified more than thirty-two thousand descendants of Johann Michael von Nida, the first of our ancestors to cross the Atlantic. As names have changed through marriage, it's hard to gauge how many of those descendants are still with us. Mr. Nida's current book is out of print, but I have been in contact with him through a Nida Yahoo group. Much of my research is in accord with his and in a few areas we disagree. Three hundred years after the voyage on the ship *Hampshire*, who is to say who's right? I've done my best to present facts accurately and to honor those who paved the way for the rest of us.

For recent family history, my brothers Don Vanness and Ron Van Ness filled in details of their boyhoods and stories involving our relatives living in Covington, Virginia. I'm grateful to Elliot Fenander for helping me research von Nida ancestry. Mark Magiera, brewmaster at Bobcat Café in Bristol, Vermont, shared his expertise of beer brewing and whiskey distilling. Thanks go to Steve Parson, who told me his story of making moonshine Marine Corps style. Much gratitude is due our Fern Forest Treehouse B&B guests who left their experiences with me and to Charles Maynard, who told me with gusto about the *Țuică* he drank in Romania. Nick Cowles was kind enough to tell me the story of his grandfather's still in Shelburne, Vermont. Gracious thanks go to Nana Lampton for hosting a party at her beautiful farm, where I learned about moonshine in Kentucky. Mountains of gratefulness to my writing groups—Mary Harwood, Michele Patenaude, Joan Zipco, Carolyn Webster, Laurie Decesare, Mary Dingee Fillmore, Spencer Smith, Shannon Anton, Sally Baldwin, Dora Coates, Khenmo Drolma, Tina Scharf, and Harriet Szanto for their careful eyes in critiquing drafts of this book. Jacqueline Tuxill performed the yeoman's work of copyediting the manuscript. My editor Reagan Rothe believed enough in the manuscript to launch its publication, for which I am grateful.

Hundreds of internet sites and magazine articles have been invaluable in my research. Books that I've gone to time and again include *The Wettest County in the World* by Matt Bondurant, *The Great Moonshine Conspiracy Trial of 1935* by T. Keister Greer, *Moonshiners and Prohibitionists: The Battle over Alcohol in Southern Appalachia* by Bruce E. Stewart, *Spirits of Just Men: Mountaineers, Liquor Bosses, and Lawmen in the Moonshine Capital of the World* by Charles E. Thompson, and *Chasing the White Dog: An Amateur Outlaw's Adventures in Moonshine* by Max Watman.

Most loving thanks to my husband Harrison Reynolds, who has developed a southern twang to his Boston enunciation and who has never ceased believing in me.

ABOUT THE AUTHOR

Louella Bryant is winner of the *Southwest Writers Award* for Nonfiction, the Premier Award for Fiction, the *Silver Bay Children's Literature Award*, the *Ralph Nading Hill Award*, and the *Vermont NEA Civil Rights Award*. Her stories, essays, and poems have been included in anthologies and magazines. She lives in rural Vermont where she works as an independent editor.

Visit her website at louellabryant.com.

NOTE FROM THE AUTHOR

Word-of-mouth is crucial for any author to succeed. If you enjoyed *Hot Springs and Moonshine Liquor*, please leave a review online—anywhere you are able. Even if it's just a sentence or two. It would make all the difference and would be very much appreciated.

Thanks!
Louella

Thank you so much for reading one of our **True Crime** novels.

If you enjoyed the experience, please check out our recommendation for your next great read!

The Poisoned Glass by Kimberly Tilley

"A great read and a fascinating retelling of a long-forgotten murder,

that still resonates to this very day...

for anybody interested in the history of the Silk City!"

-Mark S. Auerbach, City Historian, Passaic, New Jersey

View other Black Rose Writing titles at
www.blackrosewriting.com/books and use promo code
PRINT to receive a **20% discount** when purchasing.

www.ingramcontent.com/pod-product-compliance
Lightning Source LLC
Chambersburg PA
CBHW070951080526
44587CB00015B/2265